HUMAN GIVENS THERAPY WITH ADOLESCENTS

HUMAN GIVENS THERAPY WITH ADOLESCENTS

A Practical Guide for Professionals

Yvonne Yates

Jessica Kingsley *Publishers*
London and Philadelphia

Figure 6.7 on p.177 is reproduced with kind permission of John Wiley & Sons Ltd.

First published in 2011
by Jessica Kingsley Publishers
116 Pentonville Road
London N1 9JB, UK
and
400 Market Street, Suite 400
Philadelphia, PA 19106, USA

www.jkp.com

Library of Congress Cataloging in Publication Data
Yates, Yvonne, 1970-
  Human givens therapy with adolescents : a practical guide for professionals / Yvonne Yates.
      p. cm.
  Includes bibliographical references and index.
  ISBN 978-1-84905-170-5 (alk. paper)
 1. Emotional problems of teenagers. 2. Emotional problems of children. 3. Adolescent psychology. 4. Adolescence.
I. Title.
  BF723.E598Y38 2011
  158'.9--dc22
                        2010029709

British Library Cataloguing in Publication Data
A CIP catalogue record for this book is available from the British Library

ISBN 978 1 84905 170 5

Printed and bound in Great Britain by
MPG Books Group

Dedicated to my husband Paul, and sons Jonathan and Joseph

ACKNOWLEDGEMENTS

To my family I would like to say thank you for all their patience and understanding over the last 15 years.

I would like to thank Joe Griffin, co-founder of human givens therapy, for initially attracting me to the approach back in 2008 at a one-day seminar; and for reading my manuscript prior to the publication of this book.

Last, my gratitude warmly extends to the people who participated in the study on which this book is based. Namely, the wonderful adolescents, in particular 'Laura', who gave permission for information from her sessions to be included as the case study in Chapter 6; the parents and school staff who generously gave their time to be interviewed; my personal tutors, Dr Catharine Atkinson and Dr Caroline Bond, for their words of wisdom; the educational psychologists who provided support in the initial planning stages of the study, especially Anne Maguire; and other staff at the local authority for donating the topic of child poverty, which is relevant at international, national, and local levels.

DISCLAIMER

CONTENTS

Figures

Tables

Boxes

PREFACE

The research on which I based this book was carried out as part of my doctorate degree in educational and child psychology at the University of Manchester, which I completed in December 2009. From September 2006, national changes were made to the training route of educational psychologists, whereby the one-year masters degree courses were discontinued and replaced with a three-year doctorate-level course. I was one of 12 members of the first cohort to enrol on the newly established course at Manchester. It was the perfect opportunity for me to not only train to work with children and adolescents on qualifying, which I feel my career path was naturally leading me to, but also to engage in substantial research activities, which was of equal attraction. My background was considered atypical from the usual student on the course, as my work experiences up to that point had been in clinical, forensic, and community settings with child, adolescent, youth offender, adult, and older adult service-users.

My work and training allowed me to develop the confidence to work therapeutically with young people, and planning and delivering therapies was the most exciting and professionally satisfying element of my job. Over the past several years, I had the pleasure of working with a number of talented, committed, and enthusiastic clinical, forensic/clinical, and educational psychologists. Shadowing opportunities, supervision, conferences, and peer support activities ignited and maintained my passion in the field of emotional well-being and young people. It was due to the range and depth of these experiences – the people I met, and the support I received – that I felt enchanted by this area of work, which ultimately led to my research on human givens therapy for my doctoral thesis.

This book was written for a number of reasons. First, because I wished to disseminate the findings of my evidence-based research, and convey the usefulness of the approach to audiences, that go beyond educational psychology and the world of academia. Second, because there was a lack of published, accessible workbooks for professionals to use therapeutically *with adolescents* which focused on a needs-based model. Third, because although a great introduction had been made by Joe Griffin, co-founder of the human givens approach, during a seminar he delivered for trainees on the Doctorate in Educational and Child Psychology course, there was expressed uncertainty by several of them as to its uniqueness, as strategies from other therapeutic models, such as Motivational Interviewing and Cognitive Behaviour Therapy, were recommended.

This book will teach the reader how to assess adolescents' emotional needs from a human givens perspective, and how to structure the therapeutic process. The creativity that the approach lends itself to should be attractive to those who wish truly to address each individual adolescent's idiosyncratic needs, and provide a professional challenge for themselves. Ideas for practice are included but are by no means exhaustive, and it is advisable that training is sought from the Human Givens Institute (www.hgi.org.uk).

ABOUT THIS BOOK

Chapter 1 starts by providing details of the interest shown by both national and international organizations on adolescent well-being. This is followed by a brief glance at prevalence, type of psychological difficulty, and impact. The adolescent population as a special group is considered next, followed by experiences posing a threat to their development. The topic of trauma is given a large slot in Chapter 1, due to its importance as a precipitating factor, which can trigger the onset of a psychological problem. Leading on from this are coping and dysfunctional strategies; and particulars on what exactly it is about therapy that works, drawing on the research by Lambert (1992). The chapter ends with a review of different settings in which adolescents may engage in therapy; and the qualities required of those professionals who may be in a position to assist them with their emotional and psychological needs.

Chapter 2 looks at human givens values, principles, and goals, and the very important needs and resources which are key to emotional well-being. Its distinctive contribution to understanding adolescent emotional well-being includes descriptions of the human givens RIGAAR and APET models followed by their use with adolescents. RIGAAR is an acronym for Rapport building, Information gathering, Goal setting, Agreeing a strategy, Accessing resources, and Rehearsal. APET is an acronym for Activating event, Pattern perception, Emotions, and Thoughts.

Chapter 3 focuses on identifying and assessing the adolescent's human givens needs. Potential questions are included for use with young people, their parents or carers, and significant adults in school. The first figure in the chapter offers professionals with a means of recording the needs; and details of assessment measures of emotional symptoms are provided.

Chapter 4 gives an outline of RIGAAR and how to address each stage of the process. Following this, interventions are suggested that may address the Activating events, inappropriate Pattern perceptions, Emotions, and Thoughts as described by the human givens APET model.

Chapter 5 explores interventions that may be suitable in addressing each of the human givens needs. Suggestions for practice are provided for use within the therapy sessions, and during consultations with parents/carers, and significant adults in school.

Chapter 6 outlines the case of an adolescent I have worked with, Laura. Included in this section is background information about Laura; session by session records; and outcomes in relation to the research questions posed. The chapter ends with a detailed exploration of the number of sessions that may be most useful when delivering human givens with adolescents.

For ease of reference, throughout the book I have used the male pronoun for a single, unspecified person.

PART I: ADOLESCENTS AND EMOTIONAL WELL-BEING

Chapter 1

ADOLESCENTS AND EMOTIONAL WELL-BEING

ORGANIZATIONAL INTEREST

The emotional well-being of young people has recently attracted attention from a range of organizations, which may be partially due to a report on child well-being in rich countries by the world's leading children's charity organization, UNICEF (2007). Since the establishment of the Innocenti research centre in Italy in 1988, the organization has put much effort into acquiring information on the emotional well-being of children and young people around the world, with the aim of educating people on issues relating to children's rights. In their Report card 7 on child well-being in rich countries, where opinions were collated from the world's most advanced economies comprising 21 member states of the Organisation for Economic Co-operation and Development (OECD), areas were identified where societies could improve in supporting every child and young person to reach their full potential. It is significant that concerns were raised about the subjective well-being of young people in the UK. Overall, the findings of the study revealed that children in the UK ranked in the bottom third group for subjective well-being. This was the key driver of the study on which this book is based.

There is evidence in support of UNICEF's UK findings regarding high levels of children's and young people's poor emotional well-being (Collishaw *et al.* 2004). However, other studies assert that there have been no differences in either prevalence or proportion of mental disorder in children between 1999 and 2004 (Green *et al.* 2005), which may be due to differing methods of data collection, and the researchable elements of children's and young people's emotional well-being. The key factor is that many children experience poor emotional well-being, and we have a duty to address their needs.

A new coalition government took office in the UK on 11 May 2010. Its Department for Education has a responsibility to support the well-being of children and young people, including those who need targeted mental health support.

The previous UK government, with its Department for Children, Schools and Families (DCSF), showed a keen interest in children's and young people's emotional well-being with the emergence of a system for measuring and monitoring well-being, the Every Child Matters (ECM) Outcomes Framework. It is central to the drive in reducing child poverty, and remains enshrined in legislation. It has five indicators, which are Be Healthy, Stay Safe, Enjoy and Achieve, Make a Positive Contribution, and Achieve Economic Well-Being. The original green paper was published by the Department for Education and Skills (DfES) (DfES 2003).

In September 2010, ministers outlined plans for a new mental health strategy. The intention is to shift the emphasis in assessments of the quality of the NHS, by putting mental health outcomes alongside physical health indicators. The National Service Framework for Children, Young People and Maternity Services Standard 9 (NSF), published by the Department of Health (DH) in 2004, established clear standards for promoting the mental health needs of children and young people, and for providing high quality services to meet their needs (DH 2004). The NSF remains current but will need to be considered in conjunction with the new mental health strategy when it is published.

The three-year (2008–11) national Targeted Mental Health in Schools (TaMHS) programme, which is now in clusters of schools in all local authorities (LAs), was developed to test the effectiveness of evidence-based mental health support in schools for identified children, young people, and families. Schools delivering TaMHS commission a range of services procured from voluntary, charitable, and statutory organizations to meet the particular needs of their pupils, including counselling support (DCSF 2008).

Emotional well-being is also a high priority in the National Healthy Schools Programme, having been established in 1999 as a joint DH and DCSF initiative (DH 2004). One of the four themes concentrates on the emotional health and well-being of children and their families, which contributes significantly to all five ECM national outcomes for children and young people. Most schools in the country now have a range of support in place to meet the mental health needs of children and young people by being members of the National Healthy Schools network.

The healthy schools enhancement model, developed in 2009, aims to build on existing good practice and better address local priorities and needs identified by the LA and primary care trust in their local plans.

PREVALENCE

Reviews of major epidemiological studies have revealed prevalence rates of emotional difficulties in adolescents; different types of anxiety experienced by adolescents; and the potential impact of such psychological problems on adolescents' future lives. Figures have indicated that the overall prevalence for anxiety disorders in children and adolescents is approximately 6–10 per cent, and more boys are affected than girls (Carr 2006). The most common anxiety conditions found in adolescents are generalized anxiety disorder, panic disorder, and social phobia. In pre-adolescents, separation anxiety, selective mutism, and simple phobias are more common. Furthermore, the presence of anxiety disorders in childhood increases susceptibility to anxiety and mood disorders in adulthood. Thus, one may argue that there may be much to gain from providing therapeutic interventions to young people.

During my own research, I found that it was a difficult task for school staff to decide upon which four secondary pupils they would propose to be participants in my study. To explain, the number of emotionally needy pupils, as determined by school workers, exceeded my capacity as a researcher-cum-therapist, in terms of the time which I had been provided with to conduct the research, which included delivery of the human givens therapeutic approach.

ADOLESCENTS: A SPECIAL POPULATION

Adolescence is regarded by many as a period of incredible change in terms of biological, psychological, and social behaviour. There is a general consensus that adolescence occurs anywhere between 10 years and 19 years of age, as advised by the World Health Organization (WHO) (WHO 1993), and is a developmental phase between childhood and immaturity to adulthood and maturity. During this time, behaviours may compromise, sustain, or promote health-related outcomes and may indirectly influence educational engagement and psychosocial development (Currie *et al.* 2004). Carr (2006) purports that particular biological changes occur in adolescence. They include the development of sexual characteristics, hormones, and physical features. Psychological change involves transition into higher levels of thinking which to some extent affects social development in adolescents including emotional regulation; morality including the awareness that motives are the criteria used to evaluate wrong-doing; identity including a greater awareness of how others perceive them and how they see themselves; and peer group affiliation.

Cognitive development

Theories of adolescent development differ according to different schools of thought. For instance, children's development may be viewed as a continuous process, or as a discrete series of stages. Piaget (1932) developed a model of cognitive development consistent with a stages approach. He asserted that the period of formal operations occurs around age 11 and is fully achieved by age 15. At this stage, adolescents' thoughts become more abstract, which permits them to reason beyond a world of concrete reality to a world of possibilities. There are two major characteristics of formal operational thought. The first, hypothetical deductive reasoning, means that, when challenged by a complex problem, the adolescent has the ability to speculate about all possible solutions before acting upon it in reality. Thus, adolescent problem solving begins with possibility and proceeds to reality. The second characteristic is propositional in nature. Adolescents are capable of concentrating on verbal declarations and evaluating their validity without making reference to real-world circumstances.

Social and emotional development

Adolescence is a period of social and emotional development. According to Carr (2006), young people between the ages of 10 and 13 show increased efficiency in using multiple strategies for independently regulating emotions and managing stress. They also develop an increasingly sophisticated understanding of the importance of social roles and emotional scripts in forming and sustaining friendships. From the age of 13, adolescents have an increased awareness of complex emotional cycles, for instance feeling guilty about feeling angry or feeling ashamed for feeling frightened. Strategies used to regulate their emotions are informed by moral beliefs, that is, a sense of right and wrong, and impression management, whereby they engage in self-presentation strategies to deal with emotional self-disclosure in making and maintaining friendships.

EXPERIENCES POSING A THREAT TO DEVELOPMENT

Family organization

Young people may be at risk of developing a psychological problem if they live through particular experiences. For example, when family breakdown occurs, young people may be more likely to have poorer psychological and social adjustment (Jablonska and Lindberg 2007). In the two years following a divorce, boys tend to engage in behavioural problems, and girls tend to experience emotional problems. Both sexes may experience difficulties in learning, and relationships with family, school, and friendship groups. With parents who have divorced, between 20 and 25 per cent of children suffer long-term psychological problems. In contrast, 4 to 23 per cent of children from intact marriages demonstrate similar problems (Carr 2006).

Attachments

Dysfunctional attachments may also be instrumental in causing psychological difficulties in young people. In one study, poor familial relationships were mirrored in suicidal ideation and behaviour in adolescents. Parents were described in terms of conflict, abuse, criticism, tension, and instability. Adolescents felt isolated but craved an intimate connection to others; they could not make friends easily and often found themselves in deviant peer groups; they had difficulty expressing themselves; and were the victims of bullying (Bostic and Everall 2006). This is consistent with Bowlby's (1988) theory of attachment and the making and breaking of affectional bonds. In support, some agree that young people need to belong, and finding a peer group to affiliate with may meet that need, but this must not be at the expense of losing their individual identity, personal goals, and aspirations (Carr 2006). To achieve a group identity, adolescents must be able and allowed by parents and carers to grasp opportunities safely, and engage in social activities. If they are not accepted into a peer group, they may experience alienation and, in the longer term, may have difficulty developing the social support networks that are important for emotional well-being and psychological health.

TRAUMA

Definitions, causes, and types of trauma

The National Institute of Mental Health described trauma as a normal reaction to an extreme event (Public Health Emergency (PHE) 2005). Boscarino (1996) asserted that it is not necessarily the event itself that causes trauma, but a person's thoughts, feelings, beliefs, and experience of that event. Others describe the development of emotional or psychological trauma as exposure to an incident in which there is a threat to survival and adaptation (Silove, Steel and Psychol 2006). Shaw (2000) highlighted two different types of trauma. First, event trauma, which is a sudden, unexpected stressful event that is limited in its duration and geography, such as a fire or a hurricane. Second, process trauma, which is continued exposure to a long-lasting stressor, such as war or physical abuse.

Trauma may result from experiencing a specific stressful event, or exposure to a long-standing stressor. Coping with the effects of trauma may lead to social isolation; deterioration in academic performance; and behavioural problems among others, which may lead to a decline in the adolescent's quality of life and functioning (Eckes and Radunovich 2007). Adolescents are attempting to realize a sense of identity and some may engage in risky behaviours; experience relationship difficulties with their parents; and feel wide-spread emotions (Hales and Yudofsky 2003). Yet due to behavioural issues that accompany adolescence, people may discount or minimize the emotional needs of this population. Hence, it is crucial for parents, teachers, community leaders, and others in contact with adolescents to be alert to their needs, especially in times of crisis, stress, and trauma.

Crane and Clements (2005) asserted that trauma has a potentially damaging effect on the adolescent population, as significant physical and emotional growth occurs during this stage of development. For example, there is an increase in brain development, and there is evidence that emotions associated with traumatic events are capable of changing major structural components of the central nervous system and neuroendocrine system.

Adolescents experience a great deal of change, and therefore, are especially vulnerable to the effects of trauma. They are at risk of trauma-related bullying and embarrassment in school; violence in the home and community; experimentation with drugs; and other risk-inducing situations (Shaw 2000). Development may be significantly impaired and there may be long-lasting effects (Eckes and Radunovich 2007).

Assessment of trauma

In assessing trauma-related symptoms, professionals look for a presence of fear and anxiety, sleep disturbance, physical complaints including headaches or stomach pain, antisocial behaviour, depression and sadness, and fear of separation from loved ones (Boscarino 1996). According to Briere's (1995) *Trauma Symptom Checklist for Children*, the following items are indicators of posttraumatic stress: bad dreams or nightmares; scary ideas or pictures that just pop into my head; remembering things that happened that I didn't like; going away in my mind trying not to think; remembering scary things; feeling scared of men; feeling scared of women; can't stop thinking about something bad that happened to me; remembering things I don't want to remember; and wishing bad things had never happened.

Following a traumatic event, a person may avoid the feared stimuli both internally and externally. External stimuli include objects and events that serve as reminders of the trauma. Key internal anxiety-provoking stimuli include repetitive intrusive memories, thoughts, images, and emotions during waking hours and sleep (Carr 2006).

Interventions for adolescents who have experienced trauma

There used to be consensus among professionals that debriefing, for instance critical incident debriefing, was the appropriate intervention to address emotional distress immediately following a traumatic event. However, recent research suggests that this may be ineffective and may hinder the natural recovery process (Roth and Fonagy 2006). To explain, some people manage their distress best by using distraction and avoidance; therefore coercing them to talk about a traumatic event may prohibit their ability to heal naturally.

Others, namely Villalba and Lewis (2007), have asserted that individual counselling has led to improvement in symptoms of traumatized adolescents. For example, Cognitive Behaviour Therapy (CBT) involving discussion of thoughts and emotions in addition to re-experiencing the traumatic event has been found to be effective in treating adolescents who have been exposed to trauma.

Others believe that counselling which keeps a person trapped in the past does not help, and that a brief intervention, such as the Rewind technique, is more effective (Griffin and Tyrrell 2007). This element of the human givens approach is described later in the book. Another therapy, eye movement desensitization and reprocessing, also features as being helpful in recovery from trauma (Roth and Fonagy 2006). Some may also benefit from the use of medications, such as antidepressants or anti-anxiety medication, and preliminary evidence suggests that propranolol may be useful in relieving trauma symptoms (Vaiva *et al.* 2003).

ADOLESCENTS AND COPING STRATEGIES

Carr (2006) asserted that the degree to which adolescents can regulate their emotions and contemplate solving their troubles effectively depends on their capacity to manage the specific defence mechanisms and coping strategies that are available to them. Once a psychological problem has developed, it may be maintained at an individual level by psychological factors. Poor beliefs about emotional regulation and associated skills might include a negative view of self-efficacy, dysfunctional attributions, cognitive distortions, immature defence mechanisms, and dysfunctional coping strategies (Abramson, Seligman and Teasdale 1978; Bandura 1997; Friedberg and McClure 2002; Stallard 2002; Zeider and Endler 1996). In stressful situations, these beliefs, or schemas, increase vulnerability to the development of psychological problems.

The construct of coping strategies derived from the cognitive-behavioural school of thought (Zeider and Endler 1996). Coping strategies may be drawn upon to manage some situations, for instance when stressful demands outstrip available resources. There are three well-known coping strategies, including: problem focused, the aim of which is to problem solve; emotion focused, the aim of which is to regulate mood; and avoidance focused, the aim of which is to avoid the source of stress. There are both functional and dysfunctional coping strategies for the three distinctive categories; several ways in which to assess the strategies being used by individuals; and targeted interventions for professionals to use.

In a study by Van Vlierberghe and Braet (2007) on dysfunctional schemas and psychopathology in obese adolescents, overeating was considered a dysfunctional coping strategy that could be categorized as avoidance focused. The authors commented that overeating in their obese sample was a means of dealing with negative emotions that arose from dysfunctional schemas including social isolation, shame, and failure to achieve, and supports previous research by Waller (2000). Furthermore, there was a strong relationship between schemas and type of psychopathology. For instance, internalizing problems were most closely associated with social isolation and vulnerability to harm or illness. Externalizing symptoms were strongly related to the schemas connected to entitlement, and dependence or incompetence.

The findings of the study highlighted the importance of collecting data from multiple sources, as there was low agreement about the level of distress of the adolescents as reported by themselves and by their parents. This has also been found by other researchers (Achenbach, McConaughy and Howell 1987; Zeller *et al.* 2004).

THERAPY AND ADOLESCENTS: WHAT WORKS?

Working with adolescents on their emotional well-being can bring benefits and reduce the effects of any traumatic experiences they have been through. Furthermore, some specific therapeutic models, such as CBT, are developmentally appropriate for and accessible to young people during adolescence. These approaches have the potential to support young people who experience challenges during their adolescent development.

Although much attention has been paid to specific psychological therapies and their impact on outcomes, less attention has been paid to the other factors known to facilitate therapeutic change. This is where the human givens model is most distinctive, pioneering, and influential. It integrates rapport building into the assessment and therapeutic structure, namely the R in RIGAAR, thus optimizing its presence in an overt way. Even though it is not a linear model, the mere fact that RIGAAR starts with Rapport building does much to convey its importance in the therapeutic process. It follows that the fundamental inter-social skills involved in delivering therapeutic interventions effectively must not be underestimated, and one should not assume that abiding by a manualized therapeutic approach, or simply relying on the therapeutic technique, will be effective in itself.

In support, researchers have speculated that other factors, known as 'common factors', account for as much as 85 per cent of change during therapy and that the specific therapeutic approach is as little as 15 per cent only (Lambert 1992).

MEDIATORS OF CHANGE

Extratherapeutic change

Lambert and Anderson (1996) asserted that client variables account for as much as 40 per cent of therapeutic change, and include the severity of the problem, and the client's motivation to change, capacity to relate, ego strengths, psychological mindedness, and ability to identify a key problem. Therefore, not everyone who attends therapy will have a successful outcome. Consider the male adolescent who is dragged reluctantly to the CAMHS clinic by his mother. Is he going to be a willing participant in therapy? Is he going to be motivated to work on any issues he might have? Is the problem a problem to him, or just to his mother? On the other hand, we can predict that an adolescent who has expressed concern about his mood, and wanting help, will achieve more gains from therapy.

Furthermore, clients who believe that therapeutic change was largely as a result of their efforts enjoy higher levels of change, and maintenance of gains. A useful term for this is 'taking the lead'. We will see in Chapter 6 how this factor was instrumental to the change that Laura brought about in her emotional well-being, and how the choices she made equated to her belief in her capabilities of overcoming her primary problem.

Another occurrence of change can be described as 'spontaneous improvement'. This describes cases where change happens with either a minimal amount of therapeutic input, or none. A number of factors may influence spontaneous improvement, for instance the length of time the problem has existed, and the quality of social supports.

Family and social supports

In therapy with adolescents, I would argue that it is essential to meet with their primary carer, in order to assess environmental factors that may either prevent or promote and maintain change in their child's emotional well-being. Indeed, I inferred from two of my case studies that improvement was somewhat due to the influence of the adolescents' mothers. This is likely to have come from the mothers' roles in their children's therapy, that is, first, to recognize and agree with their children that they had an unmet psychological need; second, to demonstrate that their children's difficulties were important enough to them to warrant meeting with the psychologist; third, to reflect on their parent–daughter interactions during consultations, and engage in talking about their past and current ways of managing their daughters' emotional needs that had helped or not helped in the past; and fourth, to support them at home by relating in ways which had proven so far to be helpful.

In one of my case studies, the mother of the young person had reacted in the past to her daughter's emotional upset by minimizing the extent to which she felt sad, telling her to get over it, and even shouting at her. When she was asked whether any of these strategies had helped her daughter to overcome her problems, a resounding 'no' was elicited. Without lecturing the mother on the benefits of effective interaction skills, such as listening techniques, and empathy, a change happened incidentally. The mother engaged in reflection, and started to consider that she had not supported her daughter in a useful way. This vocalizing of her poor choices in ways of interacting and parenting is likely to have led to a new realization, that is, if she continued to react as she had always done, she would continue to have a superficial relationship with her daughter, and be unable to help her with her problems. She revealed that her husband achieved better results, and put this down to differences in their personalities, and own upbringings. She was the strong, stubborn-minded, resilient parent, whose mother was never seen crying, or helping others who were upset; while her husband was the calm, understanding, and accepting parent, who gave time to their daughter when she was in need, just as his father had to him.

The therapeutic relationship

As much as 30 per cent of change may be attributed to the quality of the therapeutic relationship, or 'working alliance', between client and therapist (Lambert 1992). A meta-analysis of 24 studies focusing on the relationship between therapeutic alliance and outcome was undertaken by Horvath and Symonds (1991). An impressive 26 per cent difference was found in the rate of therapeutic success, ascribed to the quality of the alliance. Focusing on therapists, it is necessary for them to set the scene of an effective therapeutic relationship, where significant progress may be achieved, by demonstrating empathy, positive regard, warmth, and genuineness. In support of these ideas Davis and colleagues found in their research that:

> the essential ingredients of effectiveness are not only the range of service options and professional knowledge and judgement, but also the human qualities of the individuals who provide these options. If they are not respectful, empathic and genuine, then little they do will be of value to families, and these characteristics can be enhanced by respectful, empathic and genuine training and supervision. (Davis *et al.* 2000, p.180)

Strupp (1980) found from a series of case studies that despite a constant therapeutic approach by the therapist, in providing the necessary conditions for therapeutic change, clients who kept the relationship on a surface level did not gain as much from therapy as those who engaged in a more meaningful relationship. Therefore, not only must the core conditions be present, which are conducive to change, and provided by the therapist, but particular personalities, maturity, motivation, and willingness to engage in therapy are also substantial contributory factors. We should not, however, think that motivation is a stable factor, as this can be subject to change, as a result of interactions with the therapist, family support, and realistic expectations of the amount of change that is likely to occur, which may be elicited from a goal setting exercise early on in therapy.

Expectancy effects

Lambert (1992) asserted that as much as 15 per cent of therapeutic change is due to expectancy or placebo effects. To explain, the mere offer of hope that emotional issues can improve is enough. In my research, adolescents' expectations of change were established. Small differences in outcomes may be viewed in these terms. Namely, that the young person who showed greatest improvement in emotional well-being asserted that she expected a positive result. However, it is not as simple as this, as this participant also had arguably the best support system, from her family and friends; and her emotional problem was the clearest to identify.

Therapeutic techniques

As aforementioned, Lambert (1992) asserted that specific therapeutic models account for a slim 15 per cent of change. Therefore, I think that what is important, when deciding upon which approach to use with adolescents, is appeal and usefulness to their uniqueness as individuals, and the emotional problems they are experiencing. Furthermore, it is necessary to establish details of any previous attempts to assist the young people with their emotional needs, by enquiring about past therapy, with whom it took place, and for how long. This would give an indication of whether a new approach would need to be adopted, perhaps in order to successfully engage the client; maintain his motivation; and allow his expectations to be refreshed.

A specific technique which has been found useful when looking at behavioural change in adolescents is Motivational Interviewing (MI) (Atkinson and Woods 2003; Aubrey 1998; McNamara 1998; Miller, Westerberg and Waldron 2003). MI has been described as a 'directive, client-centred counselling style for eliciting behaviour change by helping clients to explore and resolve ambivalence' (Rollnick and Miller 1995, p.8). MI and human givens therapy are compatible as both are client centred, involve the setting of goals, and require clients' commitment in order for change to occur. Relaxation techniques have effectively treated adolescents with anxiety disorders (PHE 2005); those experiencing pain (Larsson, Daleflod and Hakansson 1987; McGrath and Holahan 2004); and those with heightened emotional arousal (Griffin and Tyrrell 2007). Adolescents who have anxiety and depression, or who have self-harmed, may be helped by Cognitive Behaviour Therapy (CBT), which is recommended by the National Institute of Clinical Excellence (NICE) (NICE 2005).

CBT is a brief therapy that allows exploration of challenges that people face on a daily basis and facilitates understanding of the connection between thoughts, feelings, and behaviour (Dunsmuir and Iyadurai 2007). CBT has been found to improve daily functioning in those who presented with anxiety, fear, poor coping skills, negative thoughts, and depression (Kendall 1994); and obsessive compulsive disorder symptoms, social phobia, generalized anxiety disorder, and separation anxiety (Benazon, Ager and Rosenberg 2002; Siqueland, Rynn and Diamond 2005).

HUMAN GIVENS THERAPY WITH ADOLESCENTS

The human givens approach has a great deal to offer to adolescents, but further research may be required to help people to adopt its use with this population. In my study in which three adolescents engaged in therapy for emotional needs, improvements were found in their well-being (Yates and Atkinson in press). This was due not only to the human givens therapy, but to other factors that therapeutic practitioners are aware of, including extra-therapeutic change; the therapeutic relationship; and expectancy factors as previously mentioned. In addition, consultations with caregivers were seen as partially instrumental in changes in relationships, and the way they managed their daughters' behaviours and emotions, which were at the core of the young people's problems.

THERAPY IN SCHOOLS

There is a paucity of literature on therapy in schools, both in availability, quality, and effectiveness. Therefore, as therapy is being delivered in these settings, it is important that the gap in knowledge is addressed. In support of this claim, Professor Cooper (2009) reviewed the provision of therapeutic counselling in British secondary schools. Thirty studies were identified from a comprehensive literature search, on the basis of 19 counselling in schools projects. Typically, UK provision focused on humanistic, person-centred models, as opposed to cognitive-behavioural approaches adopted in schools in the United States.

Results found that young people were almost three times more likely to be referred by pastoral care teachers than by any other source, and attended on average six sessions. Clients had a mean age of 13 and there were more females than males. Family issues tended to be the area of concern among the females, and anger among males. Around 60 per cent of clients began counselling with 'abnormal' or borderline levels of psychological difficulty. Difficulties had been present for six months, and were at a severe level.

Every evaluation dataset indicated significant improvements between pre- and post-counselling. Talking and being listened to was the 'most helpful' factor identified by the clients, and pastoral care teachers were very positive about the intervention. However, although there was an indicator of the amount of change from pre- to post-counselling in the participants, no indicators were provided of change with a similar group of young people who did not have counselling, that is, a 'control' group. Thus, it could be argued that adolescents engaging in counselling improved their emotional well-being as a result of factors apart from the actual therapy. Thus, Cooper advocated the use of randomized controlled trials (RCTs) in further studies in order to reject claims that improvement in emotional well-being in adolescents was due to extraneous factors.

Cooper *et al.* (2010) conducted such an RCT, and found that counselling was not effective in bringing about improvements in emotional symptoms in young people, and could not therefore be accepted as an alternative intervention to CBT for depression. However, improvements were achieved in prosocial behaviour, and there were some indications of greater efficacy for more distressed young people.

Jenkins and Polat (2005) asserted that 75 per cent of secondary schools in England and Wales provide a counselling service. Of the 172 LAs in England and Wales surveyed on their counselling provision on an individual therapeutic basis, data suggested that there was much variation in providers and related conditions. Providers included the LA; external counsellors paid on either a sessional or voluntary basis; external counsellors employed on teachers' conditions of service; external agency staff under agreement or contract; and members of teaching staff and other combinations of services, for instance CAMHS and the European Social Fund. There was also considerable difference in the qualifications of those providing a counselling service in the secondary schools, including those with experience of teaching pupils with emotional, behavioural, and social difficulties (EBSD); educational psychologists (EPs); and counsellors with a counselling diploma. In 21 per cent of cases, levels of qualification were unknown.

Jenkins and Polat (2005) asserted that, if schools are to be seen as inclusive in their practices, counselling needs to be accessible to all students who need it, regardless of whether they fall into the category of EBSD or SEN. Inclusiveness though is dependent on other factors besides availability, such as accessibility, which is typically determined by one of two referral routes, self-referral or parental consent. Data indicated that, in 84 per cent of cases, pupils accessed the service via referral by a member of staff followed by self-referral; referral by a parent; then through a drop-in facility. Almost half the pupils were required to obtain permission from parents and a signed release from class. These requirements may affect accessibility to such services and may deter some from seeking support (Baginsky 2004; Dennison 1998; Jackson and Parnham 1996). Policies requiring prior parental consent are both inconsistent with the legal position as defined by the House of Lord's Gillick decision and may exclude those wishing to explore sensitive family issues and relationships within a counselling setting (Wheeler 2006). The data also indicated that the perception of the role of school counselling services by educational professionals varied greatly.

A number of implications were suggested to the main stakeholders, including schools, LAs, pupils and parents, regarding future developments in this area, including the minimum qualifications for counsellors; confidentiality; accessibility to pupils; and funding. The researchers suggested that there was not a well-established, consistent, and standardized counselling system across England and Wales, although there were a few LAs that had established counselling provision within their authorities, such as the counselling service established by Dudley LA (Colligan 1999).

Schools as unique organizations

Many of the adequately researched interventions have been delivered in a clinical context, and an understanding of how delivering them in a school context impacts on schools and families is desirable (DCSF 2008, p.17).

The Department for Education and Skills stated in their publication *Promoting Children's Mental Health within Early Years and School Settings* that, for most children experiencing mental health problems, it is appropriate for the additional support that they require to be met within the school setting, for instance by more specialist professionals such as EPs or other child and adolescent mental health professionals (CAMHS) (DfES 2001). However, the report alluded to the work of EPs as being assessment-led, and one-to-one therapeutic work being taken up by mental health specialists outside or only sometimes in school. At local authority level, many CAMHS workers work with schools to both assess such needs and treat them. However, due to the rise of mental health difficulties in children and young people, with prevalence rates from 12 per cent upwards, as Davis *et al.* (2000, p.170) comment it would be unrealistic to:

> expect current specialist child and adolescent mental health services to cope with significantly increased demand. Resources are already inadequate, as indicated by long waiting times. Their distribution is highly variable (Goodman 1997) and not related to need (Kurtz, Thornes and Wolkind 1994).

The authors of the paper went on to say that major increases in resources at this level were unlikely due to financial constraints and insufficient training facilities, for example in clinical psychology. In addition, personnel from education, social services, and the voluntary agencies may potentially be used to address young people's mental health needs.

In support of role expansion for EPs, researchers enquired into the possibility of EPs undertaking therapeutic work in schools (Farrell *et al.* 2006). From survey data, school staff reported that they would welcome more such interventions delivered by their link EPs. Although time may have once been seen as a barrier to this work, the researchers proposed that these professionals may now take advantage of the reduction in their statutory duty and use the time to provide individual and group therapy. Schools continue to value the one-to-one work agreed by EPs, and the move towards integrated children's services across health, education, and social services offers increasing opportunities for this professional group to contribute to therapeutic provisions.

It is worrying that Meltzer *et al.* (2000) found in their survey of children and young people in Great Britain that 20 per cent had a mental health problem. Only 10 to 21 per cent received specialist help for such problems that typically continue into adulthood (Rutter, Kim-Cohen and Maughan 2006). Thus, recent governmental guidance in this area is timely. Targeted Mental Health in Schools (TaMHS) is a UK initiative, which began in 2008. Its aim is to provide guidance to commissioners of services about innovative, evidence-based mental health models that can be delivered through schools to support related needs in the 5 to 13 age group. It offers an ecological approach to promoting mental health, viewing the child not just in terms of their problems or needs, but in relation to the environments in which they belong, for instance family, peer group, class, school, and wider community (DCSF 2008).

Particular considerations are necessary when contemplating the provision of therapies in school settings. It is generally known that high schools are extremely busy places, and practitioners may spend a significant proportion of their time arranging therapeutic appointments with adolescents, in accordance with their timetable schedules. Even if dates and times have been meticulously planned, there will always be situations where appointments will not take place, for instance due to exam arrangements, besides the usual 'Did Not Attends' (DNAs) owing to pupil illness. The smooth operational planning of therapeutic sessions around forthcoming events such as exams, tests, trips, and absences for other reasons usually depends upon your relationship with the young person, or key members of school staff. Needless to say, working with this population is demanding, and wasted trips to schools can impact on the professional's motivation, and enjoyment of this type of work.

Tip: Form strong relationships with school receptionists and key members of staff.

Successful therapy in school may also rely upon the communication between the receptionist and key members of staff, that is, the person identified for sending the young person to or reminding him to go to the appointment room. Reception staff may hold the view that it is not their responsibility to locate pupils. Of course, an appointment card or letter outlining appointment dates and times should alleviate such problems, as long as the young person remembers to refer to it. Having sessions at the same time on the same day each week may help. However, if the young people or teachers do not want the same lessons to be missed, which may happen if appointments are restricted to the same time and day each week, the professional may need to be flexible and set alternate days and times, which requires greater organization on the young person's part.

Successful therapy may also depend upon the value attached to therapeutic interventions by school staff for their students. At the last moment, demands may be placed on a student to remain in a lesson rather than attend therapy.

It is often difficult to access the room assigned in school for your therapy session before the appointment time. This has implications for the smooth commencement of the session. Preparation of any materials, for instance psychometrics and seating arrangements, may need to be organized in the presence of the young person.

My research elicited a range of pluses and minuses to delivering therapy in schools. These are outlined in Tables 1.1 and 1.2.

Table 1.1: The advantages and disadvantages of delivering therapy in schools from the perspectives of adolescents

Advantages	Disadvantages
Conveniently located	May be asked by other pupils who they went to see and why
Less of school day missed	May not reveal true feelings, due to need to return to class after, or fears about confidentiality
Familiar setting may help adolescent to relax	Viewed as less important, therefore could impact on commitment to the sessions
	May be distracted by phone or bell ringing, people passing, uncomfortable seating, interruptions from staff/pupils

Table 1.2: The advantages and disadvantages of delivering therapy in schools from the perspectives of practitioners

Advantages	Disadvantages
In the community where you work, therefore not far to travel to	Depth of work – may be at surface level due to adolescent's fears of revealing traumatic experiences in school
	Practicalities – finding a private room, accessing room, working around the bell. Environmental distractions, e.g. phone ringing in same room, noise from or views of people passing the room, uncomfortable seating, interruptions from staff/pupils

THERAPY IN OTHER SETTINGS

The big issue when working with adolescents in settings other than schools rests on actually getting them there for therapy. It usually relies on the willingness and ability of a parent or carer to take their child to the appointment. So not only does the young person need to take time out of school, but his parent or carer may need to take time off work, or spend their free time transporting him, sometimes on a weekly basis for several weeks. That is, of course, if appointments are not available outside of school hours, and the place is further than walking distance or not accessible by public transport.

There are both pluses and minuses of holding therapy sessions at a venue other than school settings, and these are outlined in Tables 1.3 and 1.4, again from both adolescents' and professionals' perspectives.

Table 1.3: The advantages and disadvantages of delivering therapy in settings other than schools from the perspectives of adolescents

Advantages	Disadvantages
Can give alternative reasons as to their absence from school – keeping therapy a private matter	May require parent/carer to drive them there if middle of day
May be more inclined to share true feelings due to being in a more private setting than school	May miss school if during school hours
May be able to concentrate fully in the therapy session	May increase adolescent's anxiety due to the unfamiliarity of the setting
May believe that their emotional well-being is a more important matter	

Table 1.4: The advantages and disadvantages of delivering therapy in settings other than schools from the perspectives of practitioners

Advantages	Disadvantages
Depth of work: can access adolescent's real problems	Did Not Attends (DNAs)
Conveniences, e.g. can make young person a drink	
Room may be custom-built for therapy, i.e. sound-proofed, comfortable seating, ambience	
Do not have to work around the school bell – important when doing trauma work and relaxation	
Others at usual place of work generally acknowledge importance of uninterrupted therapeutic sessions	

SUPERVISION AND COMPETENCE IN DELIVERING THERAPIES

It is also appropriate to raise the issue of competence; for instance, are practitioners adequately experienced, competent, and appropriately trained to both deliver and supervise others in therapeutic work when they may not have been practising therapeutically on a regular basis due to a lack of appropriate opportunities? Supervision may be viewed in both general terms, which covers matters such as safeguarding, and emotional support for the practitioner, and more specific terms, which may relate to the actual therapeutic techniques applied in sessions.

For some practitioners, for instance EPs, appropriate supervision may not be available and, as a result, such work may have to be signposted to other services. Indeed, the British Psychological Society (BPS) asserts that psychologists who are seeking to develop new skills should pursue specialized training and supervision from another professional having relevant work experience. For psychologists working in therapeutic settings, supervision is an essential module of their continuing development (BPS 2006).

PART II: HUMAN GIVENS THERAPY – 'THE NUTS AND BOLTS' AND ASSESSMENT

Chapter 2

THE HUMAN GIVENS APPROACH

Human givens is a bio-psychosocial therapeutic approach, or organizing idea, developed by Joe Griffin and Ivan Tyrrell in the 1990s (Griffin and Tyrrell 2007).

THE VALUES, PRINCIPLES, AND GOALS OF HUMAN GIVENS THERAPY

Values

The human givens approach is underpinned by knowledge of:

- the nature of the unconscious mind
- the workings of the unconscious mind
- inappropriate responses which lead to trauma, anxiety, phobias, depression, and addictions
- why things go wrong.

Principles

Human givens therapy:

- is collaborative

- draws upon a range of therapies for which there is an evidence base

- recognizes the reciprocal relationship between biological processes: perceptions; affective processes: feelings; cognitive processes: thoughts and behaviours

- pays respect to affective processes in bringing about change in thoughts and behaviours as a way of reducing symptoms and improving functioning

- focuses on the here and now rather than past experiences

- defines roles for both the therapist and the client, both of whom are active participants in therapy

- is non-voyeuristic, and therefore safe

- is brief and effective.

Goals

As described in a seminar on effective counselling based on the human givens approach, the therapeutic goal is 'to relieve emotional distress quickly and help people to find ethical ways to meet their unfilled needs' (Griffin 2008, p.4).

The human givens approach aims to help others deal with problems at the level at which they originate, that is, in the subconscious part of the brain. The approach is non-voyeuristic in that experiences do not have to be shared at a great level of detail in order for them to be resolved.

HUMAN GIVENS NEEDS

Human givens therapy works on the assumption that human beings have innate needs and resources both physical and emotional in nature. When these needs are not met or when resources are used incorrectly, emotional distress and mental health problems may occur. In psychotherapy, it is the emotional needs which are of major concern (Griffin and Tyrrell 2007). I have outlined the needs in the form of the acronym CAPS, which is depicted in Figure 2.1.

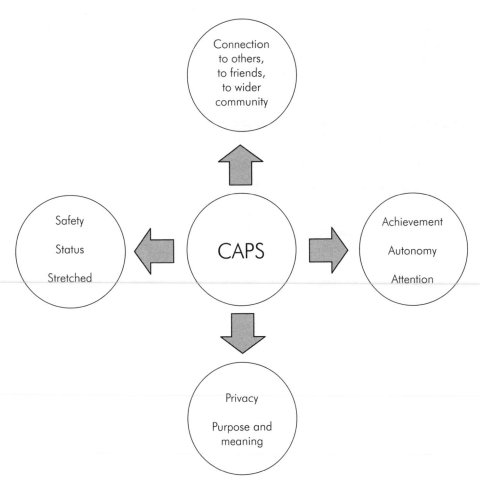

Figure 2.1: Human givens needs in the form of CAPS diagram

Others working to better understand emotional needs postulate alternative views regarding actual intrinsic needs. For example, relatedness, autonomy, and competence are concepts that are considered to take account of the essentials of the well-being of an individual (Deci and Ryan 2002). The human givens needs, connection to others, connection to wider community, friendship, attention, and privacy may all fall within the relatedness category. The human givens needs, autonomy, and competence appear to fit into the competence category, while security, status, and purpose and meaning seem to stand alone. They are, however, highly important in their contribution to an individual's well-being, and unmet needs in these areas can threaten relatedness, autonomy, and competence. The Emotional Needs Audit (ENA) tool was developed by the co-founders of human givens therapy, for the purpose of assessing needs. The ENA form can be downloaded from www.hgi.org.uk.

For the purpose of this book, although comments may be made as to close ties between particular human givens needs, they will essentially be addressed on their own.

HUMAN GIVENS RESOURCES

Within the human givens school of thought, those whose needs are well met in the world do not have mental health problems and better integrate with other people. Those whose needs are unfulfilled suffer distress and may develop mental illness, and/or, as a means of coping, involve themselves in antisocial behaviour (Griffin and Tyrrell 2007). The human givens resources that nature has provided us with may be viewed in Figure 2.2.

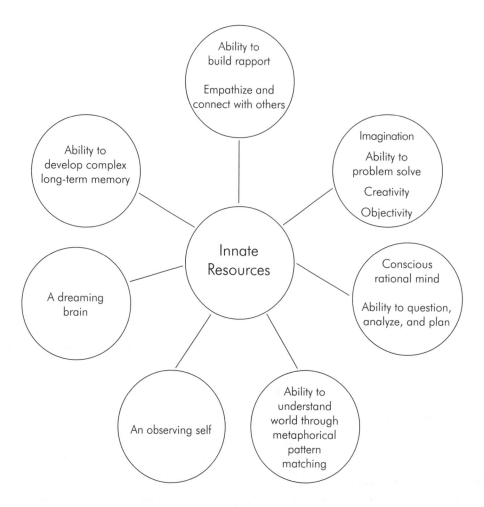

Figure 2.2: Human givens innate resources

DISTINCTIVENESS AND PROMISING CONTRIBUTIONS OF HUMAN GIVENS THERAPY

RIGAAR

A combination of factors makes human givens therapy unique. It involves therapeutic processes typical to other psychotherapies already and included in the RIGAAR model. They relate to Rapport building; Information gathering; Goal setting; Agreeing a strategy; Accessing resources; and Rehearsal. As aforementioned, rapport building is built into the assessment and therapeutic structure, and is a major contributor to therapeutic change according to several eminent researchers (Bachelor and Horvath 2006; Lambert 1992; Rogers 1976).

Agreeing a strategy, or collaborating with the client on ways to address an issue, and adapting to their preferred learning styles, thereby providing opportunities for greater autonomy, may be quite different to that of more directive approaches, such as CBT. Although a less directive approach to therapy may be desirable and assist in the creativity of the approach on the one hand, on the other hand it may prevent professionals having the confidence to apply the approach to the emotional issues that young people bring to therapy. Therefore, it is hoped that the creation of a professional's practical guide, such as this, or therapeutic manual on human givens therapy should facilitate its use.

Griffin (2008) asserted that no-one can be told how to do therapy, and the RIGAAR model indicates essential components within which the therapist and clients are free to choose strategies to address the client's unmet emotional needs.

The APET model

LeDoux (1998) highlighted the following:

- The brain works through a rich pattern-matching process.

- Emotions precede thoughts – all perceptions and all thoughts are 'tagged' with emotions.

- The higher the emotional arousal, the more primal the emotional pattern that is engaged.

Therefore, therapeutic techniques that address each of these areas may be considered to be instrumental in producing change. Griffin (2008) proposed the APET model and advocated that strategies may be introduced at each of the Activating event, Pattern matching, Emotion, and Thought levels.

ORDER OF EVENTS IN BRAIN FUNCTIONING

Neuropsychological research about the order of events in brain functioning has revealed that emotions precede reason and perception and hence some emotional responses and memories may be formed without any conscious thought (LeDoux 1998). Therefore, the co-founders of the Human Givens Institute argue that it is the emotional arousal that *causes* black and white thinking (HGIPRN 2009).

It is widely known that evidence-based CBT is underpinned by the premise that the opposite occurs, that is, thoughts precede emotions. However, arguably, and in line with LeDoux's (1998) findings, and the APET model which drew upon them, there are a great number of things that practitioners may do before challenging faulty thinking, as this may be too taxing to begin with for young people. Each of the categories in APET indicates different levels at which one may intervene. For instance, A involves exploration of the activating agent or environmental stimulus, just as in Ellis's (1991) model of cognitive therapy. For example, changes in the environment may be necessary in order to alleviate emotional difficulties. Information regarding the stimulus is consumed by the senses and is processed through the pattern-matching part of the mind (P) where meaning is attributed to stimuli based on innate knowledge and past learnings as a result of our interactions with the environment. Here, metaphors and visualization methods may help to change perceptions. The perceptions are then tagged with an emotion (E), whereby arousal may be reduced through relaxation techniques; which may lead to particular thoughts (T), which, in turn, reframing techniques may address in order to help the person re-appraise situations in a less self-defeating light. Greater details of interventions which address each part of the APET model are included later.

Pattern matching is particularly emphasized in the human givens literature. It is explained that people understand the world unconsciously through patterns or templates in the brain, and it is the strength of the emotional reaction held in the amygdala that maintains patterns. They need to be held in an incomplete metaphorical form to enable us to look for something that is crucial for our survival, which is similar to something we have been programmed to recognize. In other words, our brains are constantly matching what is new to what is already known, even though it may be inappropriate to the current circumstances (Griffin and Tyrrell 2007). For example, if one was attacked at night in the dark while walking home and footsteps were heard just before the attack, any circumstance involving any aspect of the stimuli from that event, for instance hearing footsteps while with a friend in the daytime, may lead to a faulty pattern match, and arouse intense fear in the person. Thus, one may interpret a situation as threatening even if there is no danger. Such a faulty conditioned response interferes with a normal response.

To re-programme the pattern match, the amygdala needs to be persuaded that a particular template is no longer necessary for the person's survival.

One technique that is used by human givens practitioners to address pattern-matching difficulties is *Rewind* and this will be described later in the book.

The emphasis on inducing relaxation before rehearsing strategies may also be a distinguishing feature of human givens therapy. Certainly its prominence in the Rewind technique, which is specifically aimed at de-traumatization, is indicative of a unique approach.

In summary, human givens therapy is distinctive from other psychotherapies, as there is great emphasis on rapport building, and reducing emotional arousal before any work addressing thinking patterns is attempted. It provides the practitioner with a specific technique to help those experiencing emotional difficulties as a result of a past trauma; it allows for adaptability to different learning styles presented by clients; and it advocates the use of strategies that focus on the individual's strengths, while teaching their applications to real-life situations through the use of visualization, metaphorical language, nominalizations, and humour.

HUMAN GIVENS THERAPY AND ITS USE WITH ADOLESCENTS

Human givens therapy is an effective intervention for children and young people, as it is the therapeutic process and reference to neuropsychological findings which are unique to the human givens approach, not necessarily the therapeutic techniques applied. Thus, as there is already a substantial evidence base for CBT, relaxation therapy, MI, and Solution-Focused Brief Therapy (SFBT) with children and young people, the techniques from these approaches may be tailored according to the age of your clients, in abidance with the evidence for varying age samples. The Rewind technique, a specific de-traumatizing strategy, has elements in its delivery of relaxation induction which are, however, distinctive to the human givens approach.

EXPLAINING THERAPEUTIC MODELS TO YOUNG PEOPLE

In human givens therapy, an explanation of the assessment and therapeutic process, the RIGAAR model, and levels at which interventions may be focused, that is the APET model, may be necessary if we are to truly engage the young person in therapy. However, in the human givens literature, it is not obvious that this is a key task. Literature on other psychotherapeutic approaches, for instance CBT, suggests that it is necessary to 'sell' the therapeutic model to clients in order to provide a basic understanding of the nature of treatment. This is termed 'socialization' and typically involves educating the client about the therapy; discussing his own role; and presenting the case conceptualization, that is, details of the assessment and identified therapeutic goals (Wells 2003). The aims of socialization are:

> laying the foundations for a psychological explanation of presenting problems, providing a general rationale for understanding the content of treatment, and providing accurate expectations concerning the type and level of patient involvement in the treatment process. (Wells 2003, p.46)

In addition, there appears to be no mention of relapse prevention in the human givens literature. Knowing about this concept, I encouraged the participants in my study at the end of their sixth session to refer to the work that they had completed throughout therapy. It was expected that this might help them to prevent relapse, when they become inevitably faced with future situations that evoke challenging emotions.

RIGAAR: THE APPLICATION OF THE HUMAN GIVENS APPROACH BY PROFESSIONALS

Due to the eclectic nature of human givens therapy, it may be quite daunting for professionals attempting to follow RIGAAR for the first time. However, movement between each stage in RIGAAR is quite effortless, though I am curious as to which point the therapist should introduce psychoeducation on the brain. This is such a key feature in human givens therapy, as it is asserted that emotions occur before thoughts, an idea that is distinctly different to generally accepted therapeutic models, such as CBT. This omission may lead to missed opportunities by others who are not as educated in the underlying principles and origins of the human givens approach. For instance, having a basic understanding of brain processes from this viewpoint enables professionals to deliver interventions in an order which optimizes a positive outcome. Perhaps a more serviceable name for the therapeutic framework is RIGPAAR, with P signifying the psychoeducation element. Thus, I would argue that, just as rapport building is afforded an explicit mention, psychoeducation relating to the brain ought to be too.

INFLUENCE OF PSYCHOLOGICAL PARADIGMS ON HUMAN GIVENS THERAPY

There is a lack of shared understanding about how best to help people, as there are believed to be at least 400 different therapy models available throughout the world. Undeniably, useful insights from therapies in their primitive stages of development have been needlessly complicated by an abundance of complex educational materials.

With a mounting evidence base, another distinctive contribution that human givens can make to therapy is in the assimilation of core understandings of emotional health problems as explained by other therapies, and their associated limitations. In addition, the human givens approach recommends particular strategies consistent with LeDoux's (1998) neuropsychological findings.

Freud's (1912) psychoanalytical psychotherapy

- *Understandings*: Much of our daily behaviour is controlled by unconscious processes.

- *Limitations*: Outcomes are limited by the lack of an evidence base; unrealistic models of human functioning and psychology; and a lack of acknowledgement of cultural aspects.

Behaviour therapy

- *Understandings*: Replacing unhelpful behaviours with more rewarding ones leads to improvements in outcomes.

- *Limitations*: Rejects the importance of values and meaning in life and removes autonomy.

Client-centred therapy

- *Understandings*: Listening to people's problems with a respectful and non-judgemental approach can help them overcome them.

- *Limitations*: More support is necessary in order to lower people's emotional arousal to enable clear thinking, which may involve training in social skills, anxiety, or anger management, or de-traumatization of a past experience influencing their current behaviour.

Cognitive therapy

- *Understandings*: Helping people to question the evidence for their harmful negative beliefs using their rational minds can be effective in producing change.

- *Limitations*: The alternative view is that problems may be caused by a misuse of imagination. Thus, change may arise through facilitation of more effective use of the imagination.

Positive psychology

Positive psychology is at the heart of the human givens approach. As Seligman (2007) suggested, psychologists need to pay attention to building upon strengths rather than having a preoccupation with repairing things that have gone wrong in people's lives. In agreement, Richards, Rivers and Akhurst (2008) reported that positive psychology is concerned with the study of strengths, and happiness, which has been defined as positive emotion, or a pleasant life; engagement, or the engaged life; and meaning, or the meaningful life (Seligman 2003). It also explores resilience to negative life events.

Studies by Seligman (described in Seligman 2003) have demonstrated impressive effects of happiness on social relationships. Similarly, Richards *et al.* (2008) found favourable results from a strengths and happiness intervention in tackling bullying in secondary schools. With the latter, positive psychology contributed to school-based anti-bullying interventions by supporting pupils in the long term, and therefore was considered potentially useful as a whole school anti-bullying intervention. Seligman *et al.* (2005) found in their study that writing about three good things occurring each day, and using signature strengths in a novel way, led to greater reported happiness and less depression for a six-month duration. Finally, concepts alluding to a positive psychology paradigm nurture interpersonal qualities in young people, such as optimism, altruism, empathy, being good-natured, and patience and fairness (Carr 2004; Costa and McCrae 1992; Eisenberg *et al.* 1996; Seligman 1998).

HUMAN GIVENS THERAPY: EVIDENCE BASE

As far as I am aware, the study on which this book is based is the first empirical study to evaluate human givens therapy with adolescents. One case study was chosen to exemplify the approach, so that it may assist the reader's understanding of how human givens therapy was applied to adolescents, and provide ideas for interventions. Other research activities are being undertaken currently with adults in a variety of settings, and further details may be found on the Human Givens Practice Research website (HGIPRN 2009). Sladden (2005) stated that human givens was being delivered in the National Health Service (NHS) by practising psychiatrists, and was highlighted in the *British Medical Journal* as a newcomer on the psychotherapy block.

STUDIES INVOLVING HUMAN GIVENS THERAPY

In an interview with Sladden (2005) for the *British Medical Journal*, human givens co-founder Ivan Tyrrell asserted that the human givens methods have been repeatedly demonstrated in practice; anecdotes had been positive; and it was the remit of others to provide evidence through research.

Understanding the need to contribute to evidence-based practice (EBP), studies are currently in progress to evaluate the effectiveness of the human givens approach in a range of settings.

A study conducted between 2007 and 2008 examined the efficacy of human givens therapy in a primary care setting for 112 clients, with the assistance of three therapists in an NHS practice in the South of England. Results showed that 67 per cent of clients improved in their emotional well-being following human givens therapy.

Another two-year study was conducted between 2007 and 2009 involving 1329 clients. Human givens therapy was delivered by 30 therapists working in a range of settings in both private and publicly funded practice. Outcomes were measured over a six-month period. Researchers found that 66 per cent of clients improved in their emotional well-being following therapy.

The impressive findings from both of these studies are in line with those desired by the UK's National Institute for Clinical Excellence (NICE) and the Improved Access to Psychological Therapies (IAPT) programme that was rolled out in 2008. The aim of this initiative is to improve access to evidence-based talking therapies for people with depression and anxiety disorders in the NHS. It was stipulated that a minimum level of improvement in at least 50 per cent of those treated would be achieved (DH 2008).

TRAINING IN HUMAN GIVENS THERAPY

Interest in human givens has been shown by teachers in a range of educational settings in Somerset and Devon. There, therapists have been directly employed to work in schools, and other professionals practising from the approach have engaged in work at the systems level, in delivering training. Universities training educational and child psychologists of the future have shown an interest in the approach. In addition, I have delivered presentations relating to human givens therapy with children and young people to colleagues in educational psychology services, and professionals at regional educational psychology continuing professional development events (Yates 2008, 2009a, 2009b).

The Human Givens Institute provides training to practitioners on problems seen in the adolescent population. Courses include 'How to transform the lives of challenging children and adolescents'. Importantly, those delivering the training to professionals working with this group have a wide range of backgrounds, including psychology, research, social work, mental health, and offending.

The Human Givens Institute also provides training in a technique which they assert 'cures' phobias and traumas in a short number of sessions. The Rewind technique was adapted by human givens proponents to place further emphasis on the relaxation stage before Rewind.

EVALUATING HUMAN GIVENS

As human givens therapy may comprise strategies from a number of therapeutic approaches, and participants may decide to rehearse strategies in a variety of ways, evaluation on any large scale may be challenging. Consequently, at a time when national professional organizations are demanding empirical knowledge and findings, particular therapies such as human givens may face a dilemma (Baxter and Frederickson 2005). Yet, it is understandable that following the client's lead is one of the most important aspects in delivering any therapy, and tailoring approaches to participants' preferred ways of interacting and engaging in activities in sessions is exactly what human givens therapy entails. For example, some people may prefer simply working through their problems by talking every session. Others may prefer a more creative, kinaesthetic approach; while others may desire a combination of the two. Thus further evaluations of the therapy would need to capture the strengths of the individualized approach underpinning human givens.

Chapter 3

ASSESSMENT IN HUMAN GIVENS THERAPEUTIC APPROACHES

THE ASSESSMENT PROCEDURE: IDENTIFYING AND RECORDING NEEDS

1. Work through each of the human givens needs pages, and identify needs.

2. Record answers to the questions on the worksheets provided.

3. Record identified needs on Table 3.2, the needs chart (provided later in the chapter). An example is provided in Table 3.1.

4. Copy the identified needs, and goals when agreed upon, onto Table 4.2, the needs, goals, and interventions chart. An example is provided in Table 4.1.

It may be useful to record specific vocabulary that the adolescent uses to describe his needs rather than substituting them with your own words, as this can make discussions more meaningful and real to him.

Identifying human givens needs

This book will help practitioners assess emotional distress, and plan for and target therapeutic interventions to affected adolescents. This part of the book will examine the needs using the 'R' and 'I' bits of the human givens RIGAAR model, which is the therapeutic structure of the approach. Each of the stages of RIGAAR will be explained as we work through the book. The acronym is depicted in Figure 3.1.

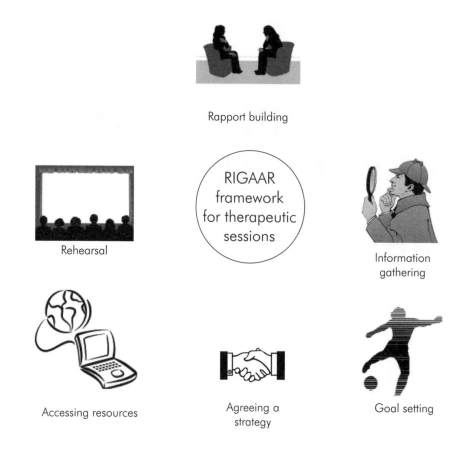

Rapport building

RIGAAR framework for therapeutic sessions

Rehearsal

Information gathering

Accessing resources

Agreeing a strategy

Goal setting

Figure 3.1: RIGAAR framework for therapeutic sessions

Rapport building

We may only get to be familiar with those needs that are most bothersome to the young person if we have first established rapport.

Empirical findings of the importance of the role of the therapeutic relationship suggest that it accounts for around 30 per cent of client improvement (Lambert 1992). Others in the field agree with the centrality of the role of the relationship in the process of psychotherapy and client change (Bachelor and Horvath 2006).

One of the core conditions required in bringing about therapeutic change as illuminated by Rogers (1976) of the person-centred tradition is unconditional positive regard (UPR). This involves acceptance, respect, and the realization that individuals are capable of autonomy. UPR may be conveyed through verbal responses, or active listening techniques, such as summarizing, paraphrasing, and reflecting, which help clients to recognize that their concerns are being taken seriously, with curiosity, and without prejudice. Non-verbal responses are also helpful, and involve matching the young person's movements; facial expressions; vocal tones; volume and speed of speech; and language used.

Although rapport building will be covered later, omitting it at this point would be foolish, as it is of great importance when it comes to obtaining accurate information. Consider the situation where a young person sits down with the professional, who is there to offer therapeutic support, and faces a barrage of questions, without first being made to feel comfortable. The fact that the two are meeting suggests that the adolescent's problems are complex, and others may have tried to help in the past, but not succeeded. He will most likely only disclose his true difficulties if he feels that he can trust the information will remain confidential, within the usual constraints, and he has faith that he will be assisted to feel better through engaging in therapy facilitated by you.

Information gathering

Effective counselling involves the obtaining of objective and accurate information to facilitate the therapeutic process. Important questions relate to when, where, and with whom did the problem start; stressors or changes occurring at that time; frequency and duration of the symptom; significant persons present or absent when the problem occurs; detailed description of the steps involved in the symptom; when it does not occur; and the person's beliefs about the problem (Griffin 2008).

Needs assessment

This part of the book looks at assessment first, guided by the human givens ENA tool (HGI 2007), which was based on an adult model. The questions have been adapted to be more adolescent-friendly. If the young person is articulate and has a good level of verbal comprehension, it may be adequate to ask the original human givens question first and see if information is forthcoming from this (see pp.56–57 for the first example of this in practice), as whatever is said first will probably convey the adolescent's true concerns. However, as I found in my research, the young people wanted clarification of the human givens needs questions. Therefore, expansion was necessary.

It is useful to gather information from a range of sources, as it usually provides a fuller picture of strengths and needs. Researchers including Van Vlierberghe and

Braet (2007) and Achenbach *et al.* (1987) postulate the necessity to collate data from other sources, as any changes in subjective well-being according to the young people's parents and tutors may support exploration of causal links. It can also help to shed light on others' beliefs about the adolescent's difficulties; expectations about his ability to make changes; the repertoire of helping approaches, which may be helpful or unhelpful; and the types and quality of support systems in place. All of these are important aspects to consider when assessing the adolescent's motivation to improve his subjective well-being. Thus, questions for parents or carers, and school staff, are also provided.

Parents/carers questionnaire

Work through the parent/carer questionnaire to ascertain the level of agreement in responses about their adolescent. If there is much disagreement, obtain further information and continue from there. As one of the human givens needs is to feel safe and secure in one's environment, the practitioner will need to ascertain whether to assess this aspect directly, that is, by working more with the parent/carer and/or other services involved with the family, for instance social care; or whether to assess the adolescent only and tailor the intervention solely to them.

School staff questionnaire

Gather responses to the human givens needs from the adolescent's teacher or adult in school who knows him best; for instance, if he has a keyworker, meet with them. Often, adults in school see a 'different' adolescent in school than is presented to parents/carers. Thus it is important to assess people from their secondary influential environment.

ASSESSMENT AND IDENTIFICATION OF HUMAN GIVENS NEEDS

In order to help you fully explore the human givens needs with the adolescent, his parent/carer, and a key adult in school, each will be described. It is always a good idea to use language that the young person understands and uses so he can provide accounts of his own reality rather than you enforcing yours, or what you believe his to be.

The assessment tool is designed to be used in a semi-structured interview format, and builds on the human givens audit as devised by the Human Givens Institute (2007). Questions are a guide only and will help you to draw out specifics of a need from the accounts of the adolescents themselves, parents/carers, and teaching staff.

Table 3.1 (on p.117) exemplifies how to complete the human givens needs chart in Table 3.2 (p.119).

CONNECTION TO OTHERS

Adolescence is a period of incredible change in terms of biological, psychological, and social behaviour. During this time, behaviours may compromise, sustain, or promote health-related outcomes and may indirectly influence educational engagement and psychosocial development (Currie *et al.* 2004). Carr (2006) purports that psychological change involves transition into higher levels of thinking which to some extent affects social development in adolescents including emotional regulation; morality including the awareness that motives are the criteria used to evaluate wrong-doing; identity including a greater awareness of how others perceive them and how they see themselves; and peer group affiliation.

The compulsion to attain intimacy with another person is so powerful that it can affect health. In fact, studies have shown that high risk factors linked to heart problems, such as smoking and diet, have less of an impact on the outcome of heart disease than whether one feels emotionally supported by another (Seeman and Syme 1987).

Although we are discussing adolescent emotional well-being here, it is important to include brief details of children's attachments, as they form the content of our internal working models, otherwise known as templates for future relationships, including those experienced in the teenage years. According to Bowlby (1969/1982), who developed attachment theory, children who have had the opportunity to develop appropriate attachments, or secure attachments, are happy, and feel able to explore their environment with increasing independence, safe in the knowledge that their caregiver will comfort and 'make things right' for them if necessary. These children are likely to grow up being loving, kind, and affectionate, and conduct themselves with confidence, cooperating well with others, and achieve well. Children who are insecurely attached are less likely to feel confident in their actions and relations with other people.

Bowlby (1969/1982) asserted that strong intimate relations happen between the first six months and three years of life between the child and significant caregiver. However, in Kennedy and Kennedy's (2004) paper on 'Attachment theory: Implications for school psychology', research was referred to that suggested that attachment could be promoted between the child and adults beyond the family environment, for instance day care providers (Howes 1999); psychotherapists (Dozier, Cue and Barnett 1994); and school teachers (Pianta and Steinberg 1992). Furthermore, in a study by Howes and Smith (1995), the positive outcomes that may arise from such attachments were outlined: children who experience positive relationships with their teachers exude greater social competence; engage in supportive relationships; have fewer behaviour problems; and demonstrate higher motivation to achieve, in contrast to peers with insecure relationships.

Risk factors associated with this need

Factors which can affect the need include:

- family breakdown
- attachment difficulties
- poor social skills.

How does the need for emotional connection to others manifest itself?

Adolescents may:

- interact inappropriately
- not have many friends
- belong to an undesirable peer group
- not be able to engage in social roles
- not be able to empathize with others
- not be able to produce emotional scripts around forming and sustaining friendships
- engage in dysfunctional coping strategies.

Questions for the adolescent

The original question posed by the human givens audit tool for this area of need is:

- Do you feel emotionally connected to others?

It is possible that the adolescent will not know exactly what is being asked if this wording is used. While it is generally better to start with a broadly focused question, some may need more guidance. This is where your interpersonal skills come into play; for instance, if after initial greetings you feel that different wording should be used other than 'emotional connection', please use alternatives instead. 'Others' refers to significant caregivers, including family members, teachers, and other day care providers. If the adolescent queries what emotional connection to others is, proceed to ask more specifically about his relationships, using the suggested additional questions that follow.

- Is there someone in your family who you can talk to about private matters?

- Do you make a point of talking about things that are bothering you?

- Do you have a best friend you can talk to about anything?

- Do you pick up easily on how others are feeling?

- Do you support your family and friends when they are troubled? How?

Questions for the parent or carer

- Can your child talk to you openly about private matters?

- Is there anyone else in the family who your child finds it easy to talk to?

- Do you make time to listen to your child when he/she needs to talk to you?

- Does your child recognize when someone close to him/her is upset?

- Does your child support family and friends when they are troubled? How?

Questions for the teacher or significant adult in school

- Has [child's name] ever talked to you about private matters?

- Has [child's name] got a special friend that he/she can talk to about anything?

- Is there a particular time during the school day when [child's name] can meet with a member of staff to discuss his/her troubles?

- Have you ever seen [child's name] comforting someone else in school?

WORKSHEET 1: CONNECTION TO OTHERS
QUESTIONS FOR THE ADOLESCENT

 Do you feel emotionally connected to others?

 Is there someone in your family who you can talk to about private matters?

 Do you make a point of talking about things that are bothering you?

Do you have a best friend you can talk to about anything?

 Do you pick up easily on how others are feeling?

 Do you support your family and friends when they are troubled? How?

WORKSHEET 2: CONNECTION TO OTHERS
QUESTIONS FOR THE PARENT OR CARER

 Can your child talk to you openly about private matters?

 Is there anyone else in the family who your child finds it easy to talk to?

 Do you make time to listen to your child when he/she needs to talk to you?

 Does your child recognize when someone close to him/her is upset?

 Does your child support family and friends when they are troubled? How?

WORKSHEET 3: CONNECTION TO OTHERS

QUESTIONS FOR THE TEACHER OR
SIGNIFICANT ADULT IN SCHOOL

Has.............................ever talked to you about private matters?

Has.............................got a special friend that he/she can talk to about anything?

Is there a particular time during the school day when.............................
can meet with a member of staff to discuss his/her troubles?

Have you ever seen.............................comforting someone else in school?

CONNECTION TO THE WIDER COMMUNITY

After bonding with a significant caregiver, the next stage is to connect with people in our family circle, then outside, with people in the community. People *need* other people in order to function in their everyday lives. Cooperation is the key! We can be affected by people who show us warmth and kindness. People who are happier and healthier tend to be those who have strong support networks of family, friends, or community. Furthermore, it is one's perception of being unloved and isolated that highly affects well-being (Hafen *et al.* 1996).

Risk factors associated with this need

Factors which can affect this need include:

- moving to a new neighbourhood

- living in an area with a poor sense of community

- living in a remote area.

How does the need for connection to the community manifest itself?

Adolescents may:

- retreat to their bedrooms

- engage in long hours on computer social-networking sites

- present at child and adolescent mental health services with issues of 'loneliness' or 'belonging'

- present at a counsellor's office in school.

Questions for the adolescent

The original question posed by the human givens audit tool for this area of need is:

- Do you feel connected to some part of the local community?

This question may be asked, but if answers are not forthcoming, proceed to ask more specifically about the adolescent's connection to the wider community, using the suggested additional questions that follow:

- How do you like to spend your free time?

- Do you feel part of your neighbourhood?

- Do you engage in any out-of-school activities?

- Do you belong to any clubs?

- Do you have friends close by?

Questions for the parent or carer

- How does your child like to spend his/her free time?

- Does your child take part in community activities?

- Is your child a member of a club in the area?

- Does your child have friends close by?

Questions for the teacher or significant adult in school

- Are there opportunities for [child's name] to join school-organized after-school clubs?

- Does [child's name] have friends who attend any school-organized after-school clubs?

- Does [child's name] attend social events organized by school staff, for instance annual festivals, fundraising events, end-of-year school discos, and school trips?

- How do school staff recognize and positively support pupils' contributions to and connections with the community?

WORKSHEET 4:
CONNECTION TO THE WIDER COMMUNITY
QUESTIONS FOR THE ADOLESCENT

 Do you feel connected to some part of the local community?

 How do you like to spend your free time?

 Do you feel part of your neighbourhood?

Do you engage in any out-of-school activities?

Do you belong to any clubs?

Do you have friends close by?

WORKSHEET 5:
CONNECTION TO THE WIDER COMMUNITY
QUESTIONS FOR THE PARENT OR CARER

 How does your child like to spend his/her free time?

 Does your child take part in community activities?

 Is your child a member of a club in the area?

 Does your child have friends close by?

WORKSHEET 6:
CONNECTION TO THE WIDER COMMUNITY

QUESTIONS FOR THE TEACHER OR
SIGNIFICANT ADULT IN SCHOOL

 Are there opportunities for.............................to join school-organized after-school clubs?

 Does.............................have friends who attend any school-organized after-school clubs?

 Does.............................attend social events organized by school staff, for instance annual festivals, fundraising events, end-of-year school discos, and school trips?

 How do school staff recognize and positively support pupils' contributions to and connections with the community?

CONNECTION TO FRIENDS

 Just as with the need to feel emotionally connected to others and the community, being able to make friends and maintain friendships is core to a person's development. In addition to emotional development, this human givens need is closely tied to behaviour, learning, and social development. If an adolescent does not have friendships, it is likely to have a negative impact on his school attainment; he is likely to have a poor understanding of social roles and emotional scripts in making and maintaining friendships, a poor awareness of reciprocal emotional self-disclosure in making and maintaining friendships, poor self-esteem as a result of imagining how others view him, he may experience daily feelings of isolation and rejection, and his physical health may be affected.

Studies have found that young people who enjoy good peer relationships also have good emotional connections with their caregivers, and those showing detachment from peers have insecure attachments with their caregivers (Howe 1995). During adolescence, the quality of friendships become highly important, and young people make preferences for more intimate peer relationships over quantity of friendships.

Risk factors associated with this need

An adolescent experiencing problems with connections to friends may:

- be a victim of bullying

- be someone who bullies others

- have poor rapport-building skills

- have poor social skills.

How does the need for friendship and intimacy manifest itself?

The adolescent may:

- intimidate peers into hanging out with him

- be a 'follower' of others who have been rejected by a positive peer group

- be on his own at unstructured times of the school day, e.g. break times

- be withdrawn and quiet in group work in class.

Questions for the adolescent

The original question posed by the human givens audit tool for this area of need is:

- Do you feel emotionally connected to friends?

If the adolescent queries what emotional connection to friends is, proceed to ask more specifically about his friendships, using the suggested additional questions that follow:

- Do you have friends at school?
- Can you talk to at least one of them about anything you like?
- Do any of your friends go to your house to hang out?
- Do you have friends outside of school?
- Are you concerned that you don't have enough friends?
- Do any of your friends get you into trouble?
- Who would you talk to if you were worried about being pushed into things by your friends?

Questions for the parent or carer

- Does your child have many friends?
- Do you know most of your child's friends?
- Are friends of your child welcome to spend time at your home?
- If your child wants to meet up with one of his/her friends outside of school time but can't do it alone, how do you help him/her?

Questions for the teacher or significant adult in school

- How does [child's name] spend his/her break and lunchtimes?
- Who is [child's name] friends with?
- What support is available in school to help [child's name] make and maintain friends?

WORKSHEET 7:
CONNECTION TO FRIENDS
QUESTIONS FOR THE ADOLESCENT

 Do you feel emotionally connected to friends?

 Do you have friends at school?

 Can you talk to at least one of them about anything you like?

 Do any of your friends go to your house to hang out?

Do you have friends outside of school?

 Are you concerned that you don't have enough friends?

 Do any of your friends get you into trouble?

 Who would you talk to if you were worried about being pushed into things by your friends?

WORKSHEET 8:
CONNECTION TO FRIENDS
QUESTIONS FOR THE PARENT OR CARER

 Does your child have many friends?

 Do you know most of your child's friends?

 Are friends of your child welcome to spend time at your home?

 If your child wants to meet up with one of his/her friends outside of school time but can't do it alone, how do you help him/her?

WORKSHEET 9:
CONNECTION TO FRIENDS

QUESTIONS FOR THE TEACHER OR SIGNIFICANT ADULT IN SCHOOL

 How does .... spend his/her break and lunchtimes?

Who is .... friends with?

What support is available in school to help............................make and maintain friends?

ATTENTION – GIVING AND RECEIVING

Receiving attention

 People seek attention in so many ways because they *need* attention. Adolescents seek opportunities to draw attention to themselves by wearing particular clothes; carrying out a good deed which affords public admiration; being the best dressed at a social event; or telling the most jokes in their circle of friends. Everybody feels special when they receive positive attention, but when attention is lacking for positive behaviours, attention for negative behaviours will do.

Proof of the importance of attention comes from a well-known experiment involving the instrumental factors in improving productivity at the Western Electric Company's plant in Hawthorne, USA. The researchers of the study were expecting to find different levels of productivity as a result of different working conditions, such as lighting, and working hours. However, what in fact occurred was improved productivity as a result of the amount of attention that the workers were being paid. The finding, known as the Hawthorne effect, indicated that paying attention or showing interest in the work of your employees increases motivation and subsequently output (Mayo 1933).

Paying attention

Our need to give our attention is just as important. For example, it is through paying attention to people in our family, friends, and other circles that we feel able to take on the values of our role models, their morals, and habits. Paying attention to others' needs helps to form reciprocal relationships, which serve to facilitate mutual exchanges of privileges. Paying attention to others also helps to maintain our place as a member in those groups.

Risk factors associated with this need

Adolescents with problems meeting this need may experience the following:

- not being recognized for doing a good job

- poor motivation

- family or peer problems.

How does the need for attention manifest itself?

Adolescents may:

- be less able to act and react in a manner that is appropriate to a situation
- not try as hard as previous efforts were ignored
- behave in ways to draw attention to inappropriate behaviours, increasing their vulnerability
- sign up to a cult, which provides attention in exchange for group membership.

Questions for the adolescent

The original questions posed by the human givens audit tool for this area of need are:

- Do you feel you receive enough attention?
- Do you pay other people enough attention?

These questions may be asked, but if answers are not forthcoming, proceed to ask more specific questions using the suggested ones that follow:

- Who gives you attention?
- What do you do that draws attention to yourself?

Questions for the parent or carer

- Does your child receive attention at home and at school for things he/she has done?
- What do you pay your child most attention for?
- Does your child give you attention?

Questions for the teacher or significant adult in school

- How does [child's name] know when he/she has done a good job?
- What does [child's name] receive the most attention for?
- Does [child's name] pay attention to other pupils?
- Does [child's name] pay attention to his/her teachers?
- Is [child's name] eager to please?

WORKSHEET 10:
ATTENTION – GIVING AND RECEIVING
QUESTIONS FOR THE ADOLESCENT

Do you feel you receive enough attention?

Do you pay other people enough attention?

Who gives you attention?

What do you do that draws attention to yourself?

WORKSHEET 11:
ATTENTION – GIVING AND RECEIVING
QUESTIONS FOR THE PARENT OR CARER

Does your child receive attention at home and at school for things he/she has done?

What do you pay your child most attention for?

Does your child give you attention?

WORKSHEET 12:
ATTENTION – GIVING AND RECEIVING
QUESTIONS FOR THE TEACHER OR SIGNIFICANT ADULT IN SCHOOL

How does .... know when he/she has done a good job?

What does .... receive the most attention for?

Does .... pay attention to other pupils?

Does .... pay attention to his/her teachers?

 Is............................eager to please?

ACHIEVEMENT AND COMPETENCE

A sense of achievement and self-competence comes from taking on challenges, and occurs with maturity, learning, and in applying skills. It is related to our need for purpose and meaning, and enjoyment of school. For example, according to a survey which asked young people to state their attitudes towards school, a probable relationship was found between liking school and educational achievement, that is, young people who like school tend to do better academically and vice versa (UNICEF 2007).

By helping adolescents to remember their successes and achievements, we tap into their personal resources which aid the therapeutic process. Accessing one's resources is a specific step in the human givens assessment/intervention structure. Once resources are identified, they may be further consolidated by their repetition through the use of guided imagery, and as a means of addressing other emotional needs.

Risk factors associated with this need

Adolescents with problems in this area could show:

- learning difficulties
- a dislike of school
- low self-esteem
- poor social skills affecting emotional well-being and hence learning.

How does the need for a sense of achievement and competence manifest itself?

Adolescents may:

- engage in disruptive behaviour in lessons
- spoil others' work
- bully others
- have a self-defeating attitude
- give up at the first hurdle
- have a greater number of absences from school than the average adolescent
- not be excited about the future.

Questions for the adolescent

The original question posed by the human givens audit tool for this area of need is:

- Are you achieving things and feeling competent in at least one major area of your life?

This question may be asked, but if answers are not forthcoming, proceed to ask more specific questions using the suggested ones that follow:

- How are you getting on at school?

- How are your grades?

- Do you enjoy school?

- What is your best subject?

- Do you think you try hard at school?

- What do you excel in outside of school?

Questions for the parent or carer

- What is your child good at?

- Do you think your child feels competent in his/her school work?

- Does your child look forward to going to school?

- When your child tells you about a piece of work he/she is proud of, how do you react?

- Do you expect your child to do well at school?

- Does your child show determination when working through challenging homework?

- What is your child interested in outside of school?

Questions for the teacher or significant adult in school

- How is [child's name] getting on at school?

- Do you think [child's name] enjoys school?

- Does [child's name] excel at a particular subject?

- What does [child's name] find particularly difficult?

WORKSHEET 13:
ACHIEVEMENT AND COMPETENCE
QUESTIONS FOR THE ADOLESCENT

 Are you achieving things and feeling competent in at least one major area of your life?

 How are you getting on at school?

 How are your grades?

Do you enjoy school?

 What is your best subject?

 Do you think you try hard at school?

 What do you excel in outside of school?

WORKSHEET 14:
YOUR CHILD'S ACHIEVEMENT
AND COMPETENCE

 What is your child good at?

 Do you think your child feels competent in his/her school work?

 Does your child look forward to going to school?

When your child tells you about a piece of work he/she is proud of, how do you react?

 Do you expect your child to do well at school?

 Does your child show determination when working through challenging homework?

 What is your child interested in outside of school?

WORKSHEET 15: ACHIEVEMENT AND COMPETENCE

QUESTIONS FOR THE TEACHER OR SIGNIFICANT ADULT IN SCHOOL

How is............................ getting on at school?

Do you think .... enjoys school?

Does............................excel at a particular subject?

What does............................ find particularly difficult?

AUTONOMY AND CONTROL

It is human nature for adolescents to move towards a state of independence, and feel that they are capable of controlling what they do to a certain extent. For instance, being able to arrange their bedrooms as they like, select which clothes to wear at the weekend, and choose who to invite over for tea are typical demonstrations of adolescents being autonomous and taking control of their lives. The term *learned helplessness*, generated by Seligman in the 1970s, describes the psychological state that typically results when one feels that events are uncontrollable (Seligman 1975). Learned helplessness is closely related to depression, and is considered to be brought about by a lack of control over situations.

Another concept that is linked to autonomy is *locus of control*, coined by Rotter in 1966, and is part of social learning theory. It refers to an individual's perception of the underlying cause of events in his life. A person with an internal locus of control attributes success to his own efforts and abilities; in other words, his actions caused the outcome. In contrast, a person with an external locus of control attributes his successes and failures to external factors such as luck or fate. It is clear to see how lack of autonomy and control may lead to distress in adolescents.

Risk factors associated with not having control

Factors which may be present for adolescents experiencing lack of control over their lives include:

- over-protective parenting – wrapping the young person up in cotton wool

- over-controlling parenting – parents taking over decisions that can be as easily made by the young person.

How does the need for autonomy and control manifest itself?

Adolescents may:

- have poor problem-solving skills

- lack persistence

- have low levels of expectations

- show learned helplessness, or a 'what's the use?' attitude

- not take responsibility for their own actions

- be fearful.

Questions for the adolescent

The original question posed by the human givens audit tool for this area of need is:

- Do you feel in control of your life most of the time?

This question may be asked, but if answers are not forthcoming, proceed to ask more specific questions using the suggested ones that follow:

- To what extent can you decide who you spend time with at home and at school?

- Are you free to take up opportunities/try a new interest?

- Do you have your own space at home?

- Who's in charge of what you wear at the weekends?

- To what extent are you free to decide how to spend your pocket money?

- How much influence do you have in setting your bed time, deciding what time to get up in the mornings, and what you eat for your meals?

- Are you allowed to try things out and make mistakes?

- Do you have control over the way you react to situations?

Questions for the parent or carer

- Does your child make decisions for him/herself?

- How much is your child's bedroom arranged to his/her taste?

- Do you have much influence over what your child wears at the weekends?

- Do you insist on things like setting times for your child to go to bed and get up?

- Do you plan meals for members of your family every day?

- Do you allow your child to make mistakes for him/herself?

Questions for the teacher or significant adult in school

- What opportunities are there in school for the pupils to make decisions in relation to learning?

- Do the pupils have their own lockers or cloak areas?

- What teaching approaches do teachers at the school use which enable the pupils to problem solve?

WORKSHEET 16:
AUTONOMY AND CONTROL
QUESTIONS FOR THE ADOLESCENT

 Do you feel in control of your life most of the time?

 To what extent can you decide who you spend time with at home and at school?

 Are you free to take up opportunities/try a new interest?

 Do you have your own space at home?

Who's in charge of what you wear at the weekends?

To what extent are you free to decide how to spend your pocket money?

How much influence do you have in setting your bed time, deciding what time to get up in the mornings, and what you eat for your meals?

Are you allowed to try things out and make mistakes?

Do you have control over the way you react to situations?

WORKSHEET 17:
AUTONOMY AND CONTROL
QUESTIONS FOR THE PARENT OR CARER

 Does your child make decisions for him/herself?

 How much is your child's bedroom arranged to his/her taste?

 Do you have much influence over what your child wears at the weekends?

Do you insist on things like setting times for your child to go to bed and get up?

Do you plan meals for members of your family every day?

Do you allow your child to make mistakes for him/herself?

WORKSHEET 18:
AUTONOMY AND CONTROL

QUESTIONS FOR THE TEACHER OR
SIGNIFICANT ADULT IN SCHOOL

 What opportunities are there in school for the pupils to make decisions in relation to learning?

 Do the pupils have their own lockers or cloak areas?

 What teaching approaches do teachers at the school use which enable the pupils to problem solve?

PRIVACY

 We all need a space in our environment in order to reflect on our experiences; to understand why we did what we did, said what we said etc.; and perhaps to learn from them so we can modify our exchanges and behaviours in the future.

Solitude and privacy go hand in hand, as people need privacy in order to enjoy solitude. This is a state of being alone without feeling lonely and can lead to self-awareness. According to researchers adhering to self-determination theory, a theory of human motivation and personality, people need to be autonomous in how they spend their quiet time, otherwise they may feel out-of-control with their lives, and have a sense of being rushed around by everybody else (Chua and Koestner 2008).

Also, researchers have found that opportunities for self-directed reflection are essential for effective learning (DeVries, Van der Meij and Lazonder 2008).

Risk factors associated with this need

Factors which can preclude an adolescent from experiencing adequate levels of privacy include:

- over-crowded living conditions
- sharing a bedroom with a sibling or siblings
- a noisy home environment.

How does the need for privacy manifest itself?

Adolescents may:

- have a poor ability to self-reflect
- have a poor understanding of their own actions
- have difficulty learning new skills
- repeat mistakes
- feel overloaded, which may impact on their attention skills and well-being
- feel out of control
- feel stressed.

Questions for the adolescent

The original question posed by the human givens audit tool for this area of need is:

- Can you obtain privacy when you need to?

This question may be asked, but if answers are not forthcoming, proceed to ask more specific questions using the suggested ones that follow:

- Do you spend time alone?

- What do you like to do when you're alone?

- How often and for how long do you like to be alone?

- Is it easy for you to find a quiet space to enjoy privacy?

Questions for the parent or carer

- Does your child enjoy spending time alone at home and doing his/her own thing?

- Is there a quiet space where your child can enjoy being alone?

Questions for the teacher or significant adult in school

- Is there somewhere in school where young people can spend time by themselves – to chill out?

- Is there somewhere quiet in school where young people can spend time by themselves, although one or two adults are present?

- Is the area known by all members of staff as a quiet area for pupils who wish to obtain privacy?

- Do school staff respect pupils' need for privacy and quiet?

- Are there particular times of the day that young people can choose to go somewhere quiet to relax?

WORKSHEET 19: PRIVACY
QUESTIONS FOR THE ADOLESCENT

Can you obtain privacy when you need to?

Do you spend time alone?

What do you like to do when you're alone?

How often and for how long do you like to be alone?

Is it easy for you to find a quiet space to enjoy privacy?

WORKSHEET 20: PRIVACY
QUESTIONS FOR THE PARENT OR CARER

Does your child enjoy spending time alone at home and doing his/her own thing?

Is there a quiet space where your child can enjoy being alone?

WORKSHEET 21: PRIVACY

QUESTIONS FOR THE TEACHER OR SIGNIFICANT ADULT IN SCHOOL

Is there somewhere in school where young people can spend time by themselves – to chill out?

Is there somewhere quiet in school where young people can spend time by themselves, although one or two adults are present?

Is the area known by all members of staff as a quiet area for pupils who wish to obtain privacy?

Do school staff respect pupils' need for privacy and quiet?

Are there particular times of the day that young people can choose to go somewhere quiet to relax?

PURPOSE AND MEANING

The need for purpose and meaning is closely related to the need to have a sense of competence, and stretching ourselves physically, emotionally, and psychologically. Human nature motivates us to seek meaningful activities which help us to learn. Any experience that is challenging and which we can learn from is 'rewarded' by the brain, which gives us a pleasure response. This allows us to repeat the experience and become even more competent at whatever it is we are trying to do. However, there is a limit to how much pleasure the brain will supply, and once an activity is mastered, effects wear off. This provides us with the incentive to seek other challenges, which may lead us towards a more purposeful and meaningful life.

Some psychological schools of thought propose that people have free will and make choices that influence their well-being. For example, humanistic psychologists such as Maslow (1943) and Rogers (1961) asserted that humans have a basic motivation towards self-fulfilment, known as 'self-actualization', which means the innate tendency to realize one's potential, and become who one can be. It involves achieving greater self-awareness about one's goals in life, and is a continuous process. Rogers advocated that people feel free when choices are available to them, and if they feel free and responsible, they will act appropriately, and participate in life.

As Rogers puts it:

> Evident in all organic and human life – the urge to expand, develop, mature… This tendency may become deeply buried under layer after layer of encrusted psychological defences… it exists in every individual, and awaits only the proper conditions to be released and expressed. (Rogers 1961, p.351)

Risk factors associated with not having a sense of purpose and meaning

The factors which can lead an adolescent not to have a sense of purpose and meaning are:

- poor motivation
- not receiving attention for trying hard
- external locus of control
- learned helplessness.

How does the need for purpose and meaning manifest itself?

Adolescents may:

- live for today

- not consider that actions today bring consequences tomorrow

- give up easily – not strive to improve

- not believe that a better quality of life can be achieved through mastery of activities.

Questions for the adolescent

The original question posed by the human givens audit tool for this area of need is:

- Are you mentally and/or physically being stretched in ways that give you a sense that life is meaningful?

This question may be asked, but if answers are not forthcoming, proceed to ask more specific questions using the suggested ones that follow:

- What is meaningful in your life?

- What is the purpose of being here on earth?

- Do you have people who need you?

- Do you have a talent that you can share with others?

Questions for the parent or carer

- What values or beliefs have you raised your child with?

- What would you like your child to achieve in his/her life?

- What do you think your child wants to do with his/her life after school?

Questions for the teacher or significant adult in school

- How is [child's name] rewarded for his/her hard work?

- How are talents and interests supported at school?

- Does [child's name] show an interest in his/her life in the future?

WORSHEET 22: PURPOSE AND MEANING
QUESTIONS FOR THE ADOLESCENT

Are you mentally and/or physically being stretched in ways that give you a sense that life is meaningful?

What is meaningful in your life?

What is the purpose of being here on earth?

Do you have people who need you?

Do you have a talent that you can share with others?

WORKSHEET 23: PURPOSE AND MEANING
QUESTIONS FOR THE PARENT OR CARER

What values or beliefs have you raised your child with?

What would you like your child to achieve in his/her life?

What do you think your child wants to do with his/her life after school?

WORKSHEET 24: PURPOSE AND MEANING

QUESTIONS FOR THE TEACHER
OR SIGNIFICANT ADULT IN SCHOOL

How is .... rewarded for his/her hard work?

How are talents and interests supported at school?

Does .... show an interest in his/her life in the future?

SECURITY – FEELING SAFE

 Feeling safe with and physically cared for by the people we live with in our youth is highly important for our emotional and psychological development. Attachment is a term relating to a secure relationship, typically with a significant caregiver (Bowlby 1969). Although attachment behaviour is typically observed in toddlers, it can also be seen in adolescents (Ainsworth *et al.* 1978). The internal working model, which refers to the early pattern of attachment between caregiver and child, is laid down in infancy, toddlerhood, and pre-school. It affects the adolescent's sense of self and his experience of others, and is a template for future relationships.

According to Howe *et al.* (1999), an adolescent with a secure attachment pattern can see himself as someone who is lovable, effective, autonomous, and competent; and others as available, cooperative, and reliable. Those with insecure attachments may see themselves as unlovable, ineffective, dependent, confused, and bad; and others as rejecting, intrusive, neglecting, unpredictable, unreliable, frightening, and unavailable.

As we grow older the need for security changes, due to the knowledge that we can effect change in our environment, and exert control over situations. Furthermore, an adolescent's need for a secure base is greater than a child's, and essential if he is to form strong relationships with others. If secure attachments have been lacking in the adolescent's life, there is still potential for him to develop an understanding of relationships. This is dependent on the influence of a warm and secure relationship with an adult (Feeney and Noller 1996).

Risk factors associated with this need

There are many reasons why an adolescent may feel insecure in his environment. Key ones are shown below.

- insensitive parenting
- family breakdown
- criminality in the family
- parental psychological problems; alcohol and substance misuse
- bereavements
- child abuse.

How does the need for security manifest itself?

Adolescents may:

- struggle to empathize

- have difficulty forming close relationships

- be uncomfortable in their own and others' company

- be controlling of others and their environment.

Questions for the adolescent

The original question posed by the human givens audit tool for this area of need is:

- Do you feel secure in all areas of your life?

This question may be asked, but if answers are not forthcoming, proceed to ask more specific questions using the suggested ones that follow:

- Do you feel safe at home?

- Do you feel safe in your neighbourhood?

- Who is important to you in your family?

- Who else is important to you?

- Who do you turn to when you are upset?

Questions for the parent or carer

- Who is important to your child?

- How competent is your child at seeking new activities and going places?

- Is there a daily routine for getting up, mealtimes, times to be in at night, and bedtimes?

Questions for the teacher or significant adult in school

- Does [child's name] have a close relationship with one of the adults in school?

- Are there opportunities for [child's name] and the adult to discuss situations, and engage in perspective taking?

WORKSHEET 25:
SECURITY – FEELING SAFE
QUESTIONS FOR THE ADOLESCENT

 Do you feel secure in all areas of your life?

 Do you feel safe at home?

 Do you feel safe in your neighbourhood?

Who is important to you in your family?

 Who else is important to you?

 Who do you turn to when you are upset?

WORKSHEET 26:
SECURITY – FEELING SAFE

QUESTIONS FOR THE PARENT OR CARER

 Who is important to your child?

 How competent is your child at seeking new activities and going places?

 Is there a daily routine for getting up, mealtimes, times to be in at night, and bedtimes?

WORKSHEET 27:
SECURITY – FEELING SAFE

QUESTIONS FOR THE TEACHER OR
SIGNIFICANT ADULT IN SCHOOL

Does.............................have a close relationship with one of the adults in school?

Are there opportunities for.............................and the adult to discuss situations, and engage in perspective taking?

STATUS

Being accepted and valued for who they are in the social groups they belong to is important if adolescents are to feel a sense of status. Status helps adolescents to maintain their personal identity, have insight into their own values while being able to take on a group identity, and play a particular role within that group. If adolescents have not enjoyed a sense of status in childhood or adolescence, they may strive to exert their power over others by dominating them through aggressive means. Loss of status can lead to depression, and is closely tied to the need for a sense of purpose.

Risk factors associated with this need

The factors which may lead to problems with an adolescent's sense of status include:

- poverty
- poor social skills
- for girls – poor empathic skills
- for boys – poor ability in sports and other physical activities
- lack of support network, both at home and in the community.

How does the need for status manifest itself?

Adolescents may:

- engage in conflict in the classroom either with other pupils or teaching staff
- affiliate with other rejected peers
- be the victims of bullying
- experience low self-esteem
- give up easily on tasks they find difficult
- demonstrate attention difficulties, which in turn may affect their learning
- have few or no opportunities to practise effective social skills within peer relationships.

Questions for the adolescent

The original question posed by the human givens audit tool for this area of need is:

- Do you feel you have status that is acknowledged?

This question may be asked, but if answers are not forthcoming, proceed to ask more specific questions using the suggested ones that follow:

- Do you belong to any friendship groups in or out of school?
- Do you feel valued by the people in the group? Do members turn to you for anything?
- How important is it to be a member of a group?

Questions for the parent or carer

- Does your child belong to any friendship groups at home or school?
- Does your child enjoy going to school?
- What activities is your child interested in?
- How is your child valued by his/her friends? Does he/she teach them anything?

Questions for the teacher or significant adult in school

- Is [child's name] a popular boy/girl at school?
- What do you think of [child's name]'s social group at school?
- What does [child's name] obtain recognition for?
- What is it about [child's name] that is valued by others?

WORKSHEET 28: STATUS
QUESTIONS FOR THE ADOLESCENT

 Do you feel you have status that is acknowledged?

 Do you belong to any friendship groups in or out of school?

 Do you feel valued by the people in the group? Do members turn to you for anything?

 How important is it to be a member of a group?

WORKSHEET 29: STATUS
QUESTIONS FOR THE PARENT OR CARER

 Does your child belong to any friendship groups at home or school?

 Does your child enjoy going to school?

 What activities is your child interested in?

 How is your child valued by his/her friends?

Does he/she teach them anything?

WORKSHEET 30: STATUS

QUESTIONS FOR THE TEACHER OR SIGNIFICANT ADULT IN SCHOOL

Is . . . . a popular boy/girl at school?

What do you think of . . . .'s social group at school?

What does . . . . obtain recognition for?

What is it about . . . . that is valued by others?

Table 3.1: Example of a completed human givens needs chart – Tom

Human givens needs	Information gathering	Adolescent's need(s) identified (tick)
Connection to others	Tom does not feel close enough to anyone to share his feelings with, and/or does not provide 'a shoulder to cry on' for anyone else.	✓
Connection to the wider community	Tom feels isolated in his neighbourhood. Free time is spent mostly by himself. He does not engage in social activities outside of home or school.	✓
Connection to friends	Tom does not feel he has enough friends, and/or a best friend with whom he can share his thoughts – feels lonely and rejected.	✓
Attention – giving and receiving	Tom feels that no-one gives him a 'pat on the back' for his efforts at school, therefore 'gives up' easily. He feigns illness when asked to hand in work he hasn't completed.	✓
Achievement and competence	Tom does not feel hopeful about the future, as he is failing to meet his predicted grades at school. He could not identify anything he is good at.	✓

Table 3.1: Example of a completed human givens needs chart – Tom *cont*.

Human givens needs	Information gathering	Adolescent's need(s) identified (tick)
Autonomy and control	Tom feels pressured by his mother to conform to house rules, e.g. meal times, clothes he should wear. He feels scared when asked to make decisions at school, e.g. the role he'd like to play in his drama piece.	✓
Privacy	Tom has no time to himself – at home, his three brothers are always around. He shares a bedroom with one of them. He feels constantly on edge and would like to have some space to think sometimes.	✓
Purpose and meaning	'What's the use of trying – no-one knows what'll happen tomorrow, do they?' Tom has no aspirations, and says no-one relies on him.	✓
Security – feeling safe	Tom feels it's too risky to sign up for badminton at the leisure centre, as it was on the news that youths had been arrested for dealing drugs ouside there.	✓
Status	Tom feels like he is 'one of the sheep' at school. He would prefer to stand out and be respected by his peers for something – but he doesn't know what that is.	✓

Table 3.2: Human givens needs chart – template

Human givens needs	Information gathering	Adolescent's need(s) identified (tick)
Connection to others		
Connection to the wider community		
Connection to friends		
Attention – giving and receiving		
Achievement and competence		

Autonomy and control		
Privacy		
Purpose and meaning		
Security – feeling safe		
Status		

OTHER INFORMATION TO RECORD

If your professional training has included assessment of emotional symptoms using psychometric measures, it will be useful to administer these at the start, during, and at the end of therapy, in order to explore severity of symptoms, and evaluate change. This is particularly important, on the one hand, when the young person has demonstrated at-risk behaviours and, on the other hand, when organizations are demanding evidence of therapeutic change, for commissioning purposes.

ASSESSMENT OF SEVERITY OF EMOTIONAL SYMPTOMS

There are a number of self-report instruments of adolescent well-being available for use by professionals. For example, the Strengths and Difficulties Questionnaire (SDQ) is a brief behavioural screening tool which measures 25 attributes including emotional symptoms, conduct problems, hyperactivity/inattention, peer relationship problems, and prosocial behaviour. There are different versions for different people. For instance, there is a self-report SDQ for 11 to 16 year olds; and informant-rated questionnaires for completion by parents and teachers. They are all freely available to download (Goodman 1997).

I requested the adolescents I worked with to complete the brief, ten-item measure, Young Person's Clinical Outcomes in Routine Evaluation, the YP-CORE, which assesses subjective well-being (Twigg *et al.* 2009). It was developed for administration by school and voluntary youth counselling service professionals. Completion of this tool each session meant it was possible to identify the variables most likely to be responsible for changes in emotional well-being at each point of the therapy, including those that occurred outside of the therapeutic sessions, for instance a betrayal by a friend.

The young person is asked to record his feelings over the last week on a five-point Likert scale, 'not at all', 'only occasionally', 'sometimes', 'often', or 'most or all of the time'.

Sessional administration

The YP-CORE or other emotional symptoms measure may be administered at the start of each session to monitor subjective well-being, and thus inform the effectiveness of the interventions being employed each week. In addition, it allows for examination of extraneous factors that may be interfering with therapy.

CHECKPOINT

You should by now have:

1. identified the young person's needs

2. recorded his needs on Table 3.2: Human givens needs chart – template

3. ascertained the severity of his emotional symptoms

4. assessed to what extent the young person is distressed.

It is important to remember that the human givens structure for therapy is not linear, and you must continue to build rapport throughout, discussing any new information that is disclosed during therapy. Furthermore, it is good practice to make an explicit connection between the young person's needs and the goals that he wishes to accomplish, in order to maintain focus and evaluate therapeutic change. Goals and interventions will be explored in the next chapter.

PART III: INTERVENTIONS AND CASE STUDY

Chapter 4

INTERVENTION STRUCTURE

RECORDING INFORMATION DURING CONTACT WITH YOUNG PERSON

Copy the needs, and add goals, interventions, and outcomes, onto Table 4.2: Human givens needs, goals, and interventions chart – template. An example is provided in Table 4.1.

INTRODUCTION

This chapter starts with a guide as to how to structure sessions with young people, following the human givens RIGAAR model. As a reminder, RIGAAR is an acronym for Rapport building, Information gathering, Goal setting, Agreeing a strategy, Accessing resources, and Rehearsal, and is depicted in Figure 3.1.

Coverage of the types of therapeutic strategies that may be useful when working within a human givens therapeutic framework follow, including CBT, MI, SFBT, and relaxation therapy.

The APET model is then described. APET stands for Activating agent, Pattern matching, Emotions, and Thoughts. This model offers a way of thinking about the order in which the brain processes information, which indicates the importance of unconscious processes in maintaining a person's emotional distress.

The chapter proceeds by exploring each of the human givens needs and appropriate interventions for each. These strategies are not exhaustive and simply offer suggestions for professionals to implement in their practice.

Evaluation

Throughout the intervention stage, evaluate the effectiveness of the strategies through consultations with the adolescents on a sessional basis, and with the parents/carers and teachers or other adults in school at least once mid-therapy and once post-therapy. The YP-CORE or SDQ may also be used with adolescents and contribute to the evaluation, as described in the previous chapter.

THE RIGAAR MODEL: STRUCTURING INTERVENTIONS

Rapport building

As aforementioned, building a good therapeutic relationship with your client is arguably the most important factor facilitating change. Rapport building is not only essential for identifying need and assessing accurately a young person's history of the distress, but is also central when it comes to working on goals, and interventions which address them. The psychoanalyst Freud (1912) was the first to describe the therapeutic alliance. Many since then have made it their key area of study (Bowlby 1988).

There are particular skills involved in building rapport, including 'pacing'. This enables the therapist to tune into the client's emotional reality and crucially allows the client to unconsciously become aware that the therapist has tuned into his reality. In addition, human givens proponents assert that 'yes sets' are effective in establishing rapport. The practitioner asks questions that demand affirmative responses, and the relationship is steered towards mutual effort in bringing about change.

Information gathering

Effective counselling involves the obtaining of objective and accurate information to facilitate the therapeutic process. Important questions relate to when, where, and with whom did the problem start; stressors or changes occurring at that time; frequency and duration of the symptom; significant persons present or absent when the problem occurs; detailed description of the steps involved in the symptom; when it does not occur; and the person's beliefs about the problem (Griffin 2008).

Goal setting

Agreeing on the therapeutic objective follows information gathering, which provides a positive focus, and determines clear criteria that may be measured by the client and practitioner. The therapeutic goal as described by the originators of human givens is to reduce emotional distress speedily, and assist clients to find ways of meeting their needs (Griffin and Tyrrell 2007).

It may be quite difficult for an adolescent to express his goals of therapy, and when asked what he would like to achieve by the end, he will often talk about the problem emotion, and say, for instance, that his goal is to not be as anxious or angry. This is where your highly honed, professional skills come into play. You have already gathered information on aspects like when the problem is better or worse. You simply now need to focus the young person's mind on specific issues that he would like to address one by one, and turn these into goals. Ensure that the goals set are positive, achievable, and related to his needs.

Agreeing a strategy

Agreeing a strategy involves ascertaining the ways in which the young person prefers to address an issue, and perhaps relates to his dominant learning style. Using this collaborative approach provides opportunities for greater autonomy, and is quite different to that of more directive approaches, such as CBT.

To exemplify, a young person might wish to examine his feelings of anger in relation to his sense of security need using a range of therapeutic activities, for instance relaxation techniques, story, and metaphor, and separating the person from the problem. However, the young person may not agree to use discussion and reframing to address the issue, which may have been suggested by the practitioner, or preferred by them. You are giving him options of how to proceed with addressing his needs. Having the adolescent take the lead in this part of the therapy may help to maintain his motivation to change, and nurture an internal locus of control.

Once strategies have been agreed upon to address the goals set, ensure they relate to the young person's identified human givens needs, then record them onto Table 4.2: Human givens needs, goals, and interventions chart – template.

Accessing resources

This area fits in well with a positive psychology paradigm. The person needs to feel positive about change, which may be promoted by helping him to remember successes and achievements; and identifying his skills and strengths. These may be repeated during guided imagery. It is essential, therefore, for the professional to know about an individual's personal resources, so that they can remind the young person to draw upon them and use them to tackle the present problem. For example, knowledge should be obtained about a person's achievements; qualities; humour; determination; when he has felt good in his life; and what he is good at.

A number of strengths may be built upon in therapy, including courage, interpersonal skills, insight, optimism, perseverance, capacity for pleasure, future-mindedness, personal responsibility, and purpose. In addition, the building of strengths helps to promote resilience and buffers against mental disorders in young people. For example, optimism buffers against depression, flow in sports buffers against substance misuse, and work ethics and social skills act as a buffer against schizophrenia (Seligman 2000).

Rehearsal

Rehearsal involves practising a strategy in therapy, such as recalling positive experiences; role play; play work; and guided imagery. Rehearsal may also be part of the young person's homework task if agreed. This takes the therapy beyond the therapy room, and helps to generalize the skill.

A particular technique that helps with the generalization of a skill is reality generation, which entails the use of people's imaginations to carry out the desired changes. For example, visualizing events and positive emotional reactions to them enables the successful rehearsal of desired behaviours. This creates a template for success in their minds, and is likely to lead to success in reality (Mindfields College 2007).

Table 4.1 below exemplifies how to complete the needs, goals, and interventions record in Table 4.2. Please note that the young person you are working with is likely to have more than one need, but probably not all the needs listed! Note that the interventions are provided only for the purpose of demonstrating how to complete the record. Greater details of interventions, and how to support their application in practice, follow in Chapter 5.

Table 4.1: Example of a completed human givens needs, goals, and interventions chart – Tom

Identified human givens needs	Goals from information gathering	Interventions	Outcomes
Connection to others	Tom would like to develop a closer relationship with his dad.	To change perceptions: Story work using metaphors or imagery and visualization	1:1
		To build skills: Interpersonal skils Role play Assertiveness training A typical day	1:1 1:1 1:1 1:1 and/or speak to Dad
Connection to the wider community	Tom wishes to spend more time outside of his home.	Assertiveness training Role play	1:1 and speak to parents and school staff
Connection to friends	Tom would like to make friends with a particular group of boys in his class. He also wants to make friends with young people in his neighbourhood.	Visualization exercise Assertiveness training Social skills Role Play	1:1 and speak to school staff 1:1 and speak to parents and school staff
Attention – giving and receiving	Tom would like school staff to recognize when he has worked hard.	Positive self-talk exercise Remark on others' strengths	1:1 and speak to school staff
Achievement and competence	Tom would like help getting 'back on track' with his school work. He would quite like to learn how to play badminton.	Relaxation exercises Time management activity	1:1 and speak to school staff and parents

Table 4.1: Example of a completed human givens needs, goals, and interventions chart – Tom *cont.*

Identified human givens needs	Goals from information gathering	Interventions	Outcomes
Autonomy and control	Tom would like make decisions more easily, and without worrying about them.	Relaxation exercises Discuss responsibilities he'd like to assume Reframing techniques Worry postponement technique	1:1 and speak to parents
Privacy	Tom would like to spend time somewhere quiet, without his brothers.	A typical day Relaxation exercise	1:1 and speak to parents and school staff
Purpose and meaning	Tom would like to feel needed by his family.	Guided imagery and visualization Discussion Tom to record details of tasks/support he's been asked to do/ provide at home Remind him of these times during a relaxation exercise	1:1 and speak to parents
Security – feeling safe	Tom would like to feel safer in his community, as he'd like to start badminton lessons.	Relaxation exercise Positive self-talk Information giving A typical day	1:1 and speak to parents
Status	Tom would like to feel valued by pupils at school, and his brothers at home.	Visualization exercise Positive self-talk Social skills practice Assertiveness training	1:1 and speak to school staff and parents

Table 4.2: Human givens needs, goals, and interventions chart – template

Identified human givens needs	Goals from information gathering	Interventions	Outcomes

INTERVENTIONS BASED ON OTHER THERAPIES

It is beyond the scope of this book to provide details of all stategies that fall within each of the therapeutic models referred to in this section. Information is generally available on each one.

Solution-Focused Brief Therapy

SFBT has been described as a departure from problem-dominated talk, thinking, and description to solution-oriented talk, thinking, and description, and is welcomed by professionals including EPs (Redpath and Harker 1998). SFBT was developed by De Shazer (1985) and has been found to be effective with child populations in school settings, and with adolescents (Durrant 1995; Metcalf 1995; Murphy and Duncan 1997; Rhodes and Ajmal 1995; Selekman 1993). This fits in with a human givens approach as, rather than dwelling on past events and distress, its focus is on generating solutions.

Motivational Interviewing

There are a number of strategies for use within the MI model, and I found that 'A Typical Day' strategy was useful during my work with adolescents. The approach as a whole has been successful with secondary school pupils (Atkinson and Woods 2003; McNamara 1998). 'A Typical Day' was described within the 'Menu of Strategies' by Rollnick, Heather and Bell (1992), and involves obtaining details from the young person about a typical day when a particular behaviour happens, and when it does not. This activity facilitates rapport building, and helps the practitioner to understand the context of behaviours and emotions. It also provides the client with an opportunity to identify best times of the day that new behaviours may be tried.

Relaxation therapy

Relaxation skills are important in helping a young person tolerate situations in which he feels threatened (Carr 2006), for instance going to parties when fearful of peer rejection, or staying in class when feeling overwhelmed with the level of work expected.

There are very few studies, however, on adolescent emotional well-being and relaxation, although much support has been established for the use of relaxation training with young people experiencing physical pain, for instance therapist-assisted and self-help relaxation programmes when administered in school settings

(Larsson *et al.* 1987; McGrath and Holahan 2004). Relaxation training is also part of CBT and is reportedly helpful during exposure to trauma-related memories (Hamblen 2010). During a relaxed state, people are typically more susceptible to suggestion; therefore remarking on their strengths and past successes during this time may help them to switch their unhelpful patterns of thinking into more constructive ones (Griffin and Tyrrell 2007). Strategies emerging from relaxation therapy include three/five breathing, progressive muscle relaxation, guided imagery, and visualization.

Narrative therapy

White and Epston are prominent names in narrative therapy. In 1990, they proposed that people develop stories, or narratives, which guide them through life. Narratives are influenced by cultural and social factors, and establish the range of possible solutions that are available to people (White and Epston 1990).

Narrative therapy offers a particular way of conversing with people, whether it is professionals who work with others, for instance adolescents, or directly as a therapeutic approach, that is, with a young person. In consultation with professionals in relation to adolescents, narrative techniques can help them to reflect on what they understand about the adolescent's situation. Positive values or intentions that are driving their actions are reflected back to the professional.

The aim of using it with young people in therapy is to help them tell their story in a non-blaming way by the use of externalizing language to separate the problem from the person. Therapy involves empathizing with the client, re-naming the problem, hearing the values he is conveying through stories about his problems, and using creative strategies to tell a different story about his problem.

Narrative therapeutic techniques have been adopted for use with children and adolescents (Vetere and Dowling 2005); adolescents with anorexia nervosa (Dallos 2003; Fox 2010); children who present with aggressive behaviours (Gollop and Pulley 2010); people with learning disabilities (Wilcox and Whittington 2003); and in consultancy with staff regarding people with severe and enduring mental health problems.

Cognitive Behaviour Therapy

CBT is a brief therapy that allows exploration of challenges that people face on a daily basis and facilitates understanding of the connection between thoughts, feelings, and behaviour (Dunsmuir and Iyadurai 2007). The core principle is the deliberation of a client's faulty thinking which leads to unhelpful feelings and dysfunctional behaviour. It involves strategies such as the positive reframing of thoughts; realistic and meaningful goal-setting; and scheduling of pleasant activities (Noble and McGrath 2008).

There is a growing body of evidence for the use of CBT with young people (Ahrens-Eipper and Hoyer 2006; Siqueland *et al.* 2005; Squires 2001). Furthermore, some researchers have found that gains have been maintained over time (Currie 2001). However, in other instances, children and young people's difficulties have returned (EBMH 2008; Ehntholt, Smith and Yule 2005). This was found by Ehntholt *et al.* (2005) in their study investigating a school-based CBT group intervention for refugee children who had experienced war-related trauma. The children's conditions had relapsed just two months after a decrease in symptoms of Posttraumatic Stress Disorder (PTSD) had been recorded. It was thought to have been due to either external circumstances or to an inadequate treatment period.

Neuro-Linguistic Programming (NLP)

The *Rewind* technique is an intervention aimed at reducing the emotional distress associated with a traumatic event. It originated from one of NLP's co-founders, Bandler (1985). Human givens proponents have developed the Rewind technique further, by placing greater emphasis on the skill of relaxing the client deeply before the technique is used, in order that the higher cortex of the observing self is in operation, and free to reframe the memory from a traumatic one into an ordinary one.

APET AND HUMAN GIVENS INTERVENTIONS

Numerous interventions are proposed by Griffin and Tyrrell to alleviate a person's mental distress, and improve functioning (2007). These are described using the mnemonic 'APET' and are outlined in more detail below.

Interventions to address *activating* events (the *A* in APET)

The first intervention concentrates on the activating event and includes removal of the stimulus, for instance dealing with the bullying that has led to the person's depression.

Professionals can:

- ask the young person how he would like to go about this

- support the young person in raising the issue with another adult, for instance a parent, teacher, other school staff member, or community worker known to the young person

- contact the adult directly on behalf of the young person and express concerns/develop a plan of action/agree to review the situation after change is implemented.

Interventions to address inappropriate *pattern* perceptions (the *P* in APET)

Inappropriate pattern perceptions were explained earlier in the book (see p.44). The interventions which address trauma follow.

HUMAN GIVENS TRAUMA INTERVENTION

Human givens therapists have developed the NLP Rewind technique in order to target traumatic memories trapped in the amygdala. This approach originated from a co-founder of NLP (Bandler 1985). In human givens therapy, greater emphasis is paid to the skill of relaxing a client deeply before the technique is used. It is safe as it does not further embed the fear by asking clients to incessantly talk about the problem, non-voyeuristic in that the client does not need to tell the professional the details of what happened, and fast, as some clients may be de-traumatized after just one session. The technique works by allowing the traumatized individual, while in a safe and relaxed state, to reprocess the traumatic memory so that it becomes stored as an ordinary and non-threatening, albeit unpleasant, memory, rather than one that continually activates a frightening response. It is reportedly effective and suitable for both children and individuals with disability (Griffin and Tyrrell 2007).

It is inadvisable to attempt the Rewind technique with a young person with a genuine problem unless 'learned and practised under the guidance of an experienced practitioner' (Griffin and Tyrrell 2007, p.384). Human givens trained therapists can be accessed via the Human Givens Institute website (HGI 2010). However, a description follows of the elements included, for reference.

ELEMENTS INCLUDED IN A REWIND SCRIPT

Arousing the emotions: You could say

> 'You don't have to tell me anything about the event for it to have an impact but it may help to get a general idea about the kinds of things that were happening there.'

The idea is to resurrect the emotions and memories about the particular situation that continues to evoke a traumatic repsonse, in order to have emotions to work with.

Normalizing the response: You could say

> 'You talk about being concerned that you may be led again into things like that if you're pressurized. This is a natural response because you've learned that saying "no" so many times didn't stop it from happening.'

Providing a neuropsychological explanation: You could say

> 'The emotional memory of that night is stuck in a part of the brain called the amygdala and our aim today is to move it into a different part so your brain knows that the memory is in the past, and the horrible emotions associated with it are also in the past.'

Increasing motivation / expectation: You could say

> 'Little by little, over the next few days, you should be feeling better about yourself, like yourself more, like you used to. It'll be possible for you to move forward and think about getting on with your life in a more positive way.'

Relaxation exercises: You could say

> 'So we're going to start by releasing tension in your mind and body.'

Consider using three/five breathing, and visual imagery (described in more detail in the emotional arousal section below).

Rewind of the traumatic event: Ask the young person to visualize a portable television set magically appearing with a video recorder. You could say

> 'You have a video of events of that night. You have a remote control. It controls everything familiar – colour, volume, speed, so you can control everything about this experience.'

The remainder of this part of the Rewind involves imagining rewinding and fastforwarding through the traumatic event playing on the tape using a double dissociation technique, where the person watches himself watching the video. It ends when the event no longer elicits a traumatic response.

Relaxing down: You could say

> 'I'm going to count down to 1 and I want you to notice with each number that you become more and more awake. 10… 9… 8… 7… 6… 5… 4… 3… 2… 1…'

Evaluation: You could say

> 'So if you were to think back to the event, where 1 is not bothered and 10 is very bothered, where are you now? When you used to think about it in the past where would you have rated it?

'What people find is that, over the next few hours, they start to feel a little better, they sleep better, they wake up in the morning and something's different. They can usually think more clearly. Rate it tomorrow and you'll probably find that it drops from… to…

'I really look forward to seeing how you've got on next week.'

STORY METAPHOR

Metaphors hold deep meanings and, when generated, offer invaluable insight into a person's perspective. In terms of therapeutic outcomes, metaphors may signify what is trying to be achieved; the resources needed; and how to proceed. Stories which I have used with children and adolescents in the past have come from the book *101 Healing Stories for Kids and Teens*, by G.W. Burns (2005). The chapters are structured in ways which help the readers to identify stories which relate to particular problems, and are aimed at particular ages.

NOMINALIZATIONS

Nominalizations, according to Griffin and Tyrrell (2007), are abstract nouns that mean different things to different people, and may have powerful therapeutic effects on clients, especially while they are in a more suggestible trance state. For instance, *power* is a nominalization. It contains no sensory information and is content free, which is the reason why it may hypnotize both the listener and the speaker. In order to make sense of them, pattern-matches are sought in order to aid meaning. It is essential for the professional to have gathered the nominalizations that the adolescent uses in his language; and noted the ones which he uses to describe himself, his aspirations, and particular experiences that have been problematic for him. An exemplary script follows from one of my case studies.

'From meeting with you, I know that you have great intelligence. Year 11 is a difficult time for everyone, especially boys who don't have the maturity that you have. They may feel pressurized into being horrible and say things that aren't true that hurt other people. They may be jealous, as you're a strong rugby player.

'Your unconscious mind has many strengths and resources that you can draw upon in different situations when you need to. You can remember your beauty, maturity, and the qualities that you share with other family members in order to overcome other people's nastiness, which will open up new possibilities and bring happiness to your life again.'

Interventions to address *emotional* arousal (the *E* in APET)

RELAXATION

One might use relaxation training to re-programme unhelpful patterns of responses, and reduce emotional arousal. Relaxation techniques may enable the person to function more intelligently; increase his positive thoughts; and reduce black and white thinking.

Figure 4.1: It's easy... just relax!

Relaxation induction

Below I outline the principles of inducing relaxation. The professional's confidence and knowledge of this area needs to be conveyed through verbal and non-verbal language in order to maintain rapport and trust.

• Take your time.

• Suggestions for inducing a trance state need to occur in time with the client's breathing, so each number counted happens on each out breath, or if the client is breathing rapidly, every second or third out breath.

- Induce relaxation further by asking the client to identify a safe place that is special to him, and engage his imagination by introducing visual, auditory, and kinaesthetic inputs in order to deepen his focus. For example, ask him what he may be hearing, seeing, feeling, and smelling, on a journey that you ask him to take while in deep relaxation, in his imagination, on his way to the special place in his mind, where he feels calm and at peace.

- Reduce the speed of your words, lower the pitch, and deepen the tone of your voice in order to match the client's experience of falling deeper into a trance state.

- Last, bring the client out of this deeply relaxed state by reversing the induction procedure.

(Griffin and Tyrrell 2007)

Three/five breathing technique

When the out breath is longer than the in breath, the parasympathetic nervous system is stimulated, which induces the relaxation response. Clients are asked to breathe in for a count of three and out for a count of five, or in for a count of seven and out for a count of eleven (Griffin and Tyrrell 2007). A three/five breathing exercise script follows, which I developed as part of my doctoral work with young people, and was based on practice taught by Atkinson during the course of my doctoral degree programme (2008).

1. Settle down comfortably where you won't be disturbed. Make sure your clothes are loose, not tight. You can sit or lie down to do this. Place your hands beside you or on your lap, and uncross your arms and legs.

2. Some people find it easier to relax if they have their eyes closed. You can do this if you wish, but you are in control.

3. Now pay attention to your feet on the floor, or your legs and arms wherever they are leaning against, and your head on the cushion, pillow, or back of the chair.

4. Many people find the easiest way to relax is by slowing their breathing down and breathing out for longer than they breathe in as this stimulates relaxation. Let's have a go.

5. Close your eyes if you wish and take in a big, deep breath and feel your lungs filling with air. Imagine inflating a big balloon that's resting on your tummy on the breath in, and deflating it on the breath out. Breathe in, and

again, breathe out. Feel the breaths flowing smoothly around your body and feel your arms and legs as floppy as a ragdoll's.

6. Start making each breath out last longer than each breath in. I'd like you to breathe in for a count of 3: 1... 2... 3..., and out for 1... 2... 3... 4... 5... This is called 3/5 breathing and helps your mind and body to relax.

7. Again, in 1... 2... 3... and out 1... 2... 3... 4... 5... You're getting the hang of this.

8. As you breathe in, breathe in comfort and warmth. As you breathe out, breathe out stress or any problems. You might like to imagine bubbles all around you with a worry in each one and, each time you breathe out, the bubbles blow further and further away until they pop.

9. In for comfort, 1... 2... 3..., and out with the stress, 1... 2... 3... 4... 5...

10. You might be feeling like your body is getting heavier, sinking into the chair or bed or floor, or lighter, like a feather, a kind of lifting sensation.

11. Isn't it lovely to relax and enjoy this, a special time just for you, just helping your mind and body to perhaps feel better.

12. Okay, I'm going to count backwards from 5 to 1 and, when I reach 1, you'll feel completely alert and very calm. 5... 4... 3... 2... 1... You can breathe deeply like this wherever you are just a few times, if you feel like you're stressed or are worried or want to burst into tears.

13. Well done, you've learned how to use the 3/5 breathing exercise in order to help your mind and body feel relaxed. If you want to stop here, remember to open your eyes for a few seconds before getting up slowly.

Progressive muscle relaxation (PMR) technique

PMR releases tension in groups of muscles. Clients are asked to tense each muscle group in turn, to induce both physical and mental relaxation. An example and a script you could use follow.

'I'm going to teach you how to relax parts of your body so that in future you may recognize when you're physically tense and can use this exercise to relax your body. It's important to only clench your muscles comfortably. Don't continue if any part of it feels uncomfortable. If you've had problems in the past from serious injuries, muscle spasms, or back problems, skip this part, because muscle tensing could make any of these conditions worse. Also, it's better to practise before meals so the technique does not interfere with your digestive processes.'

1. We're going to start at the bottom of the body and work our way up. So pay attention to your right foot now, breathe in slowly while you clench your foot muscles for 5 seconds. Let's count, 1... 2... 3... 4... 5...

2. Now let the tension go and notice how different it feels to your left foot. As you breathe out, you could say 'relax or calm' or another word that you associate with relaxation. Now do the same with the left foot, clench it... and release, feeling a warm, relaxing sensation flowing through it.

3. Now tense your right leg including your thigh, and release and slowly exhale feeling the warmth circulating around your leg.

4. And the same with the left leg, tense it... and relax.

5. Now tense your right arm, then release exhaling slowly and saying your relaxing word. The same again for your left arm, hold it, then release.

6. Now tense your right hand, feel your fingertips pressing into your palms... and relax... Notice the difference in how your right hand feels to your left hand. Let's try it with your left hand now... and relax...

7. Now tense your tummy and breathe in... and relax.

8. Now tense your chest... and relax.

9. Now tense your neck and shoulders, shrugging your shoulders up towards your ears and hold... and release breathing out and feeling a surge of relaxation flowing through your shoulders. They might feel heavier and warmer.

10. Now tense your face by screwing it up and hold for 5 seconds, breathing in slowly, then release, feeling relaxation.

11. Now, you've learned how to tense and relax your muscles and, with practise, you can release tension in the body when you need to. Just let that warm, relaxed feeling travel through your body, still concentrating on your breathing, being aware that your body is completely floppy and relaxed. If you wish to stop at this point, count backwards from 5 to 1: 5... 4... 3... 2... 1... And now

you're wide awake and calm. Remember to open your eyes for a few seconds before you get up.

GUIDED IMAGERY AND VISUALIZATION TECHNIQUES

Guided imagery involves using the imagination to reduce emotional arousal. Visualization concentrates on the rehearsal of success in the imagination. It addresses emotions relating to a particular difficult situation past, present, or future. Visualization techniques often tag onto the end of guided imagery.

I created the 'Relax your way to exam success' CD (Yates 2009c), the cover of which is depicted in Figure 4.2. It was based on the research that informed this book. The CD is available from www.ypspsychology.co.uk/Products.html and includes the script below and soft, instrumental music to facilitate relaxation. In addition, there is a three/five breathing exercise, outlined above. Purchase of the CD is not essential as visualization scripts can be tailored to the individual and his particular area of concern.

Figure 4.2: Exam stress buster

Here is a guided imagery and visualization script you could use:

1. I'd like you to sit or lie back until you're comfortable, making sure your clothes are loose, and think of a place you'd like to visit in your mind that's a special place just for you, where you can go to in your mind and be safe, happy, and calm. It might be the seaside, a country garden, a country park with fields and perhaps a lake or a stream. Wherever you can relax the best. If you don't have somewhere in mind, perhaps you've seen a picture of somewhere in a travel magazine or on the TV. Perhaps you'd like to go there.

2. So concentrate on your breathing, doing the 3/5 exercise, in for 1... 2... 3... and out for 1... 2... 3... 4... 5..., feel your body nice and relaxed, no tension.

3. While you're relaxing deeply, I'd like you to travel to that special place in your mind, you're walking towards it and it'll take a count of 20 to get there. 1... 2... 3... 4... on your way now, 5... 6... 7... you're looking forward to getting there, 8... 9... 10... 11... half way there now, 12... 13... 14... 15... 16... almost there, 17... 18... 19... 20... Excellent, you've reached your special place.

4. Now have a good look around in your imagination, what can you see? Perhaps a bright blue, clear sky or the rippling water nearby. What can you hear? Perhaps the sound of seagulls or gentle flowing water. What can you smell? Perhaps the fragrance of flowers or chocolate. How does the ground feel? Is it soft, sandy, grassy, warm, or cool? Are you warm or cool? Can you feel a gentle breeze flowing through your hair or is it absolutely still? Is the sun warming your arms and face?

5. You can choose to be alone or with someone else. And you can choose what you would like to do in your special place, whatever it is to help you to enjoy relaxing, more deeply, with every word I say.

6. If you prefer to listen to the sounds where you are and not my voice, that's fine too, as long as your mind is relaxed. You're in control of your subconscious mind, that private part of your mind where all your feelings, memories, and habits are stored. While you're comfortable and relaxed, I want you to let your subconscious mind help you to change your anxious feeling about performing your dance routine for your mock GCSE dance exam. You're giving your mind permission to learn the new emotion of feeling calm, confident, and relaxed.

7. Okay, I want you to imagine that it's the evening before your mock GCSE dance exam. You're feeling very calm. You know exactly what you need to do to pass and you're confident that you'll do well because you've practised the routines many times. Your friends know how much emotional effort you've put into taking the group dance routine and are supporting you 100 per cent. They are happy that you're taking part.

8. It's bedtime, you concentrate on packing your bag for tomorrow and go to bed at a reasonable time. Your family is happy that you're taking the mock exam tomorrow and certain that you'll participate and will do the best you can. You can relax about knowing the dance routines now and enjoy a peaceful night's sleep.

9. You wake up in the morning feeling refreshed, confident, and calm. You get dressed and have a good breakfast to help your brain concentrate well for the day ahead. It might be natural for you to put pressure on yourself to do the exam, but remember, all human beings need challenges in order to flourish and reach their potential. You're aiming to take this dance exam on as such a challenge and produce a positive outcome for yourself. You may feel like you'll let others down if you slip up, but you're not going to worry about that today. You've learned a better way of coping with your anxiety. You feel calm, confident, and relaxed. Remember when you were walking in your special place, how beautiful it was, and how relaxed you were. Wasn't that a nice feeling? You can understand that you are in control of how you feel. You can decide whether to become stressed or whether to cope with life's events. Don't worry if you start to feel a little anxious just before the exam, most people do. It may help to laugh about it with a friend or relative who's with you.

10. If the people you'll be dancing with are stressing about the exam, just let that blow past you, because you are calm and relaxed about it and you're confident that you will cope with the event without stressing or feeling tense. You are going to be focused on your moves and not what other people are thinking or feeling. You're not worrying about the exam at all.

11. It's time to walk into the dance studio now. This feeling of calm and confidence is flowing through your mind and body and you're ready to show the examiners what you can do and what you've learned. Remember that an exam is just a way of finding out if you've learned what has been taught. The music is playing in the background. Your friends give you a smile and a confident nod. You tell yourself, 'I can do this.' You might even

enjoy the dance! You perform the dance wonderfully and feel very happy with the way you coped with the event. It was worth all the preparation.

12. And now that you've learnt the new habit of feeling calm and relaxed and confident during a performance exam, you're realizing that other things that worried you before just don't seem to worry you as much any more. You're learning to cope with everything that goes on around you. Your ability to be able to relax just now when in an imaginary exam situation is proof that you can get rid of that old habit of worrying about things, especially forthcoming trips, activities, and exams. From this moment on, your subconscious mind is helping you to do things in life that you were worried about doing. Your old habits are no longer holding you back.

13. Okay, it's time to come back now, and I'm going to help you by counting from 10 to 1 and, when I reach 1, you'll feel alert but calm and relaxed. 10... 9... 8... you might like to stretch up, 7... 6... 5... you're almost back now, 4... 3... 2... 1... Gently open your eyes and take a few moments before you get up if that's what you want to do.

14. Well done for allowing your subconscious mind to banish that old habit of worrying. I expect that when you take your exams, and go on future trips, you'll be able to cope much better with the experience. After all, you've told your mind how you'd like it to work now, so it should do what you've instructed it to do.

    Relaxation exercises are intended to be practised regularly in order for full benefits to be gained from the techniques, for instance to enable people to reduce their emotional arousal quickly and effortlessly, in real-life situations, where appropriate.

Humour

Atkinson (2008) asserted that it is impossible to experience two contradictory states; therefore practising techniques which help to switch emotions may increase children and young people's chances of successfully changing future feelings of anger into less harmful responses. Of course, humans have a whole repertoire of emotions, and it is the behaviours resulting from them that may be viewed by others as problematic, but wholly appropriate in some situations.

Adolescents may use their imagination to experience more positive feelings, for instance amusement through the use of humour. I asked participants to think of a situation that they found funny and could recall without much effort. They were prompted to recall something that made them feel angry, then to switch their emotion to one of amusement by remembering the humorous event. Griffin and Tyrrell (2007) asserted that rehearsing situations vividly, for instance through people's imagination, encourages them to match these patterns in reality; and if goals have been realistic, there is a greater likelihood of changes occurring.

Interventions to address *thoughts* (the *T* in APET)

REFRAMING

You may help another to interpret experiences differently and recognize new possibilities through the use of reframing techniques from cognitive therapy. Reframing, at the simplest level, means changing a negative thought into a positive one. Tables 4.3 and 4.4, based on Greenberger and Padesky (1995), provide an example regarding a young person, Jemma, who is asked to join a group in drama class. First we have Table 4.3.

Table 4.3: Jemma's thoughts record

Situation	Emotions	Automatic thoughts	Behaviours
Jemma is asked to join others in drama class	Ashamed or angry	I'll probably freeze. I'm useless at acting – no-one wants me in their group. Everyone will laugh.	I'll pretend I'm sick and get sent out so I won't have to take part.

As a professional, you can help Jemma to reframe her thoughts by asking her pertinent questions:

- What evidence do you have that you are 'useless at acting'?
- What evidence do you have that you'll 'probably freeze'?
- What evidence do you have that the others will laugh?
- How could we find out if that is true or false?
- Can you think of any times that it might not be true?
- How would you feel if you weren't scared of acting in the group?

Table 4.4 might exhibit Jemma's responses. You will notice the addition of the columns 'Alternative thoughts' and 'Alternative outcomes'.

Table 4.4: A reframing record for Jemma

Situation	Emotions	Automatic thoughts	Alternative thoughts	Alternative outcomes
Jemma is asked to join others in drama class	Ashamed or angry	I'll probably freeze. I'm useless at acting – no-one wants me in their group. Everyone will laugh.	Some of the pupils in the group are kind, and they might help me.	I'll give it a go and see what happens.

POSITIVE SELF-TALK

Positive self-talk has good implications for people's mental and physical well-being. Self-talk, like thoughts, has the ability to trigger behaviour and affect self-esteem, as it may be based on beliefs created in early childhood (Weikle 1993). It may be useful for a young person to record his strengths, perhaps in written form, such as a list or flash cards. These are a set of cards bearing information that may aid learning and memory, and may be used to absorb information effectively (Renou 2010).

It is not unusual for a young person to get stuck at this point. Therefore, it may be necessary to help him to think about positive things about himself as one psychologist suggested in the area of resilience (Grotberg 2003). According to Grotberg, a resilient young person is one who says:

I have (e.g. I have people who love me and help me)

I am (e.g. I am a likeable person and respect myself and others)

I can (e.g. I can control myself, and generate alternative solutions to problems).

Therefore, start the adolescent off with *I have...* but be careful not to donate ideas unless absolutely nothing is forthcoming. Then, you might say that you had noticed while working with him that he has a great sense of humour, or he is cooperative, and so on.

SEPARATING THE PERSON FROM THE PROBLEM: REPLACING ANXIETY WITH HUMOUR

Separating the person from the problem, taken from narrative therapy, is a therapeutic technique which features highly in the human givens approach. With young people you can get as creative as you like. The example provided describes a drawing activity.

You could also consider clay modelling, or other artistic materials, to help young people represent the person and the problem. The aim should always be, however, to help your clients to perceive the emotional problem as an external phenomenon, and to challenge it using their strengths. Until the problem is conceptually separated from the young person, he will be unable to utilize all his resources against it.

Example

Rob was angry about a lot of things happening in his life, and had a reputation at school for being hot-headed. He could go from zero to ten at a moment's notice. For the purpose of this exercise, he was first asked to imagine an angry-looking character; draw it on one page; and give it a name. He named it 'Devil'. Second, he was asked to draw a new character, which had a temperament opposite to the first, and to give it a name. He named it 'Friend'. In comparing the two, Rob described the figures in terms of how they would move, behave, and speak; and how others would react to them. The character 'Devil' would take over Rob when competing demands were made on his time, for instance his mother asking him to feed and take his baby brother to nursery before going to school, while his friends would be waiting to walk to school with him, and give him a hard time when he was late reaching them. This set Rob's mood for the day, and he constantly got into trouble for his outbursts in class. The alternative character, 'Friend', would be seen smiling and getting on with people at school and the leisure centre. He would also be seen working out problems through talking, and asking adults to mediate if he was struggling. His teachers would show that they were proud of him, and his friends would admire him for being able to cope with multiple tasks. Rob said he preferred the 'Friend' character and he used a metaphor to explain his intentions: 'I'm gonna bury Devil.'

Chapter 5

INTERVENTIONS FOR EACH OF THE HUMAN GIVENS NEEDS

INTRODUCTION

This chapter starts with a menu of interventions, some of which may be suitable for the adolescent you are working with, and vehicles for delivery. Interventions are based on what we know works with young people from the findings of research. However, the way you deliver them needs to be tailored to the individual, faithful to the human givens tradition, and must be agreed with the adolescent. Interventions may be recorded on the assessment and intervention record.

Interventions addressing each of the human givens needs follow, and are not exhaustive by any means, but simply food for thought. The reader is reminded that, once needs have been identified, further questioning is necessary in order for specific goals within the need to be set. Thus, only general suggestions for practice can be provided, as each adolescent's particular goals differ, and with human givens therapy strategies are client-led or, at minimum, agreed with them.

Following the agreement between the adolescent and professional about how best to address his needs, and meet his therapeutic goals, an intervention plan can be developed. Strategies may be recorded on the needs, goals, and intervention chart. Before we can start this, however, it would be good to revisit the types of strategies that we know work with young people. A menu has been developed as an aide memoire and is depicted in Table 5.1.

Table 5.1: Techniques, strategies, vehicles for delivery, and creative methods

Techniques and strategies	Vehicle for delivery and creative methods
Metaphors	At the start of therapy, introduce the metaphor 'Shedding old habits' and engage the adolescent in the Falling leaves and Berry birth exercise. Make a 3D tree, and as each concern is addressed and conquered, tear off a leaf (sticker). At the same time, other trees grow berries. Add a berry (sticker) each time progress has been made (in line with pulling a leaf off the tree).
Nominalizations	Story work, guided imagery, visualization.
Humour	Language, drawings, visualization. Create a 'Giggle box' (adolescent puts in pictures, photos, and objects of things that make him laugh).
Rewind technique	Visualization method for trauma, or kinaesthetic method – run through with objects.
Relaxation	3/5 breathing, progressive muscle relaxation, guided imagery, visualization. Practise in session – use script if necessary. Record an audio CD for practice at home. Help adolescent to create a model of his favourite relaxing scene, and include tactile objects, and smells. Alternatively, help him to create his very own Zen garden, which epitomizes tranquillity and symbolism.
Reframing	Language, discussions, worksheets, drawings, writing. Help the adolescent to create a 'Filmstrip' of a situation and problematic emotions, thoughts, and behaviours, followed by another scene which offers a reinterpretation of the situation. Scan photos onto it, or draw onto it, and use speech bubbles.
Positive self-talk	Flash cards. Help adolescent create a 'Front page' of a newspaper, accentuating his achievements. Design a 3D figure on which he can stick or pin positive statements about himself. Introduce the idea of a gemstone that, when held or rubbed, can remind him of his positive attributes.

Techniques and strategies	Vehicle for delivery and creative methods
	Introduce the idea of a charm bracelet on which each bead or charm can represent a strength. One can be made in session, and items attached to it. It could be placed in a personalized treasure chest.
	Make a paper chain with the adolescent and write a strength onto each link. Suggest it is put up in a prominent place in his bedroom.
Worry postponement technique	Discussion, visualization, drawings, writing. Help adolescent to identify a soft object, like a beanie bear, and have him attach a word signifying the worrying thought to the bear, who can keep hold of it until the designated time.
	Suggest that a birthstone is kept close to the adolescent as a reminder of a generally 'worry-free' time (birth signifying a time when the adolescent's main concerns were to be fed, warm, and clean).
Activity scheduling	Timetabling pleasant and necessary activities onto a chart. Behavioural experiments; for instance, note mood after taking the dog for a walk versus mood after watching a TV programme.
Separating the person from the problem	Drawings, writing, story metaphor. Create 3D models of the dichotomous characters.
Social skills training	Role plays, scripts, story metaphor. Behavioural experiments; for instance, have the young person watch someone who socializes well with others, to pick up tips.
Assertiveness training	Role plays, scripts, behavioural experiments, story metaphor.
Conflict resolution	Role plays, scripts, story metaphor.

BEYOND THE THERAPY ROOM

Interventions can, and should, go beyond the therapy room and include other people besides the young person. For example, if a need is to have a better relationship with one's sibling, a strategy may be to liaise with parents or carers and find ways forward to help siblings enjoy being related to each other more. If a difficulty lies with others bullying the young person, working closely with his keyworker or adult who knows him best in school may be of great benefit.

It is for these reasons that the suggestions for practice that follow sometimes include interventions that you may wish to discuss with the adolescent's parents or carers or significant adult in school.

INTERVENTIONS ACCORDING TO HUMAN GIVENS NEEDS

Connection to others

Social skills – non-verbal communication in addition to verbal communication – may be what an adolescent who has difficulty connecting on an emotional level to others needs to learn.

Here are some suggestions for practice.

IN THERAPY:

- Model to the adolescent how to interact with a person he may want to get to know better, for instance giving appropriate eye contact; showing interest in the other by asking him questions; raising topics of conversation that tap into a shared interest; ending with a time for a future chat or meet-up.

- Teach empathy skills, that is, how to pick up on another person's mood and act and react sensitively to him.

- Set him the challenge of using his newly found skills of communicating, with someone he trusts, perhaps using 'A Menu of Strategies' intervention from Motivational Interviewing (see p.132).

IN CONSULTATION WITH PARENTS OR CARERS:

- Ensure they are modelling good listening techniques.

- Ask them to provide time during which they can have 'heart to hearts' with their child.

- Ask them to use comments like 'Thanks for listening to me', 'Thanks for giving me a hug when I was upset', 'Thanks for watching the film with me'.

IN CONSULTATION WITH SCHOOL STAFF:

- Provide regular one-to-ones for the young person, during which time he can practise his social skills with a trusting and trusted adult in the school setting.

Connection to the wider community

 Community can be anything outside the family circle, and can therefore be school, neighbourhood, or clubs the adolescent is a member of. A young person may be disadvantaged from accessing the wider community due to lack of funds, or poor self-confidence; therefore interventions may be usefully targeted to a practical approach.

Here are some suggestions for practice.

IN THERAPY:

- Teach assertiveness techniques if the adolescent's lack of engagement is due to poor confidence.

IN CONSULTATION WITH PARENTS OR CARERS:

- If their child agrees, could they go with him to the area's leisure centre to see if there are any activities of interest to him, and the costs involved?

IN CONSULTATION WITH SCHOOL STAFF:

- If the need is that the adolescent does not feel that he belongs to his school, find out about his specific talents and promote nurturance of them by staff and pupils. For example, if the adolescent is a good writer, photographer, or interviewer, is there a school newspaper that he could take part in publishing?

- Determine whether the adolescent could take part in any of the extra-curricular activities at school.

- If cost is an issue, are there funds to support the adolescent's participation?

Connection to friends

 Friends are more important than adults to adolescents, and have greater influence over their behaviours. Thus, teaching young people about positive peers, and how to be a good friend themselves, may help them to share values and beliefs acceptable to the majority of people. The role of the keyworker in school, or parent/carer, is important here.

Here are some suggestions for practice.

IN THERAPY:

- Complete an activity, 'What is a good friend?'

- Explore with the young person what he does when he tries to make friends with others and identify areas that can be improved.

- Role play a situation where you act as a person in the adolescent's social group, with the aim of ascertaining strengths and weaknesses in his communication style.

- Have the young person visualize a situation where he is making friends with someone for the first time using techniques from relaxation therapy.

- Model to the adolescent how to interact with a person he may want to get to know better, for instance giving appropriate eye contact; showing interest in the other by asking him questions; raising topics of conversation that tap into a shared interest; ending with a time for a future chat or meet-up.

- Teach empathy skills, that is, how to pick up on another person's mood and act and react sensitively to him.

- Set the challenge of identifying someone he would like to make friends with, and approaching him using good social skills.

IN CONSULTATION WITH PARENTS OR CARERS:

- Discuss the importance of positive friends for their child, and the possibilities for their friends to spend time at the house.

- If it is difficult for the adolescent to meet up with his friend due to lack of public transport, could they help him with this?

- Recruit the help of a significant adult in school, perhaps the adolescent's keyworker, form tutor, or teaching assistant he knows well, and ask him to engineer a friendship with appropriate supervision.

- Meet with the significant adult to check that he himself has good rapport building skills, and is able to identify positive peers for the adolescent with this need.

- Suggest that the adolescent and the proposed new friend(s) sign up to a new activity together, or are given a shared responsibility or job in school, as this may help to maintain the contact and, hence, the relationship.

Attention – giving and receiving

 It is important for young people to be able to pay attention to other people in order to build reciprocal relationships, and to receive attention for what is socially acceptable behaviour. Therefore, asking questions of the adolescent about what he craves attention for, and how he goes about it, will lead to an intervention plan to meet this need.

Here are some suggestions for practice.

IN THERAPY:

- Engineer opportunities during therapy to provide attention to the adolescent for his successes; for instance:
  - helping to build a 3D model of a brain
  - drawing beautifully, writing neatly
  - focusing his attention
  - being punctual
  - being willing to work with you.

- Ensure that the adolescent is seeking attention for appropriate behaviours.

- Ignore inappropriate behaviours where possible.

IN CONSULTATION WITH PARENTS OR CARERS:

- Discuss the importance of the attention they pay to their child for positive behaviours.

- Discuss their role in spending individual quality time with their child.

- Ensure that others notice the appropriate behaviours and comment on them to the adolescent, by informing the significant adult in school of the adolescent's wishes to behave in a more acceptable way.

- Hold a group consultation with all the subject teachers who have contact with the adolescent and advise of the importance of reinforcing positive behaviours through social praise and rewards, such as house points and positive report cards.

Achievement and competence

 Finding out about the smallest of achievements that elicit a sense of competence in adolescents is the initial stepping stone to meeting this need. It may be necessary to call on the help of others in the adolescent's life in order to help him with this. Here are some suggestions for practice.

IN THERAPY:

- During a relaxation exercise, provide nominalizations for his particular achievements.

- Ask the adolescent to write about his achievements to someone he would like to know about them.

- Ask the adolescent to share his achievements with a friend.

- Encourage the adolescent to help others who have difficulty in an area in which he is talented.

- Over-emphasize his achievements, and try to help him expand on them. For example, if the adolescent says he is quite good at woodwork, can he help make sets for school productions? It may be necessary to hold a meeting, in this case, with specific subject teachers, to enable this to happen, and to give the young person confidence in offering his services and displaying his talents to others.

IN CONSULTATION WITH PARENTS OR CARERS:

- Discuss nurturing the child's interests, even if it does not fit with their own interests. For example, if their son prefers to do trampolining than football, respect this, and nurture his motivation and pride in his ability.

- Ask the subject teacher if he would produce certificates or send home 'good news' letters or certificates to the young person and his parents/carers.

Autonomy and control

 This area of need can thwart an adolescent's personality and independence, which may impact on other areas of his development. Thus, interventions which serve to increase independence may help in multiple ways.

Here are some suggestions for practice.

IN THERAPY:

- Talk through situations with the adolescent that he has identified as areas that he would like to have greater control over.

- Ask the adolescent to write a list of the things he would like to make his own decisions on, for instance what he may wear at the weekend; and where he may visit and with whom in school holidays or at weekends.

- Use reframing techniques if the adolescent feels he is being unfairly controlled by his parents/carers. Where appropriate, convey the message that a parent's job is to worry about their children, and to alleviate that worry, some parents do everything for them.

- Help the adolescent to find other ways of being autonomous, perhaps in school.

IN CONSULTATION WITH PARENTS OR CARERS:

- Ascertain any risks or anxieties attached to allowing their child to have more control over, for instance, how he spends his free time.

- Discuss any ways in which their child can take on greater responsibility at home.

IN CONSULTATION WITH SCHOOL STAFF:

- Are there opportunities in school whereby the adolescent can be involved in making decisions over his learning, for instance, that tap into his preferred learning style?

Privacy

This area of need can prevent an adolescent from reflecting on his life, and lead to feelings of lack of control over life's events. Therefore, interventions which serve to help the adolescent experience solitary time positively may be of benefit.

Here are some suggestions for practice.

IN THERAPY:

- Ask the adolescent to identify a time every day when he can find a quiet place to enjoy solitude, and reflect on the day's events.

- Suggest a daily relaxation exercise.

- If the adolescent has trouble with intrusive thoughts, for instance thoughts that generate anxiety or low mood, teach the 'worry postponement' technique from CBT (Wells 2003). Ask the adolescent to acknowledge worrying thoughts if they occur during his solitary time, then put them to one side, metaphorically speaking, until a predetermined time when he is 'allowed' to engage with them, for instance 6.30pm every night for half an hour. Recognizing that delaying engagement with worrying thoughts may be difficult, the young person may be prompted to use his imagination to acknowledge worries in any way that he pleases. For example, perhaps 'worry' could be a word sitting on a boat that sails into port. The young person might watch it arriving, then imagine waving it off until its return at 6.30pm, as it departs moments later.

IN CONSULTATION WITH PARENTS OR CARERS:

- Talk to the young person's parents/carers about ensuring their child is able to spend time in a private space at home to engage in solitary activities.

IN CONSULTATION WITH SCHOOL STAFF:

- Establish whether there is a quiet place during unstructured times that the adolescent can retreat to.

Purpose and meaning

Human nature motivates us to seek meaningful activities which help us to learn. Therefore, interventions which help the adolescent face challenges, experience success, and promote an internal locus of control may help.

Here are some suggestions for practice.

IN THERAPY:

- Attribute success to his own efforts and abilities; in other words, ensure that the young person knows that his actions caused the outcome.

- Prompt the young person to recognize links between his motivation to undertake tasks, learning, and feelings of success.

- Set up opportunities for which you can give social praise for effort as well as outcome. For example, if educating about brain processes, consider using a simplified 3D model of the brain, which the young person can take apart and put together as you are talking him through the structures.

- Have the adolescent teach you something.

IN CONSULTATION WITH PARENTS OR CARERS AND SCHOOL STAFF:

- Discuss available opportunities for new activities to be undertaken.

- Discuss the importance of helping the adolescent to see links between motivation, persistence in tasks, and outcomes.

- Discuss the importance of social praise in maintaining a young person's interest, motivation, and persistence in activities which may help him to improve his skills, and develop new ones.

IN CONSULTATION WITH SCHOOL STAFF:

- If the adolescent has an Individual Education Plan (IEP), allow him to participate in producing the targets for academic, behavioural, social, or emotional targets.

Security – feeling safe

Feeling safe involves being made to feel lovable, effective, autonomous, and competent; and seeing others as predictable, available, cooperative, and reliable. Thus, interventions that promote healthy relationships will be valuable.

Here are some suggestions for practice.

IN THERAPY:

- For each therapy session, ensure that you arrive promptly, and *always* turn up when you have arranged to. If you are going to be unavoidably late, or need to cancel the appointment with the adolescent, contact him to give reasons.

- Always follow through on finding out things on behalf of the adolescent if this is what you have agreed.

- Teach social skills, so that the young person can form and maintain appropriate relationships.

- Teach positive self-talk.

- Ask the adolescent to produce flash cards with positive statements on them about himself.

IN CONSULTATION WITH PARENTS OR CARERS:

- Discuss different ways that they can show their love to their child.

- Discuss the importance of setting and enforcing boundaries.

- Discuss the importance of routines at home, for instance bed times.

IN CONSULTATION WITH SCHOOL STAFF:

- If individual sessions are being provided, ensure your punctuality.

- Always follow through on finding out things on behalf of the adolescent.

Status

 Being accepted and valued for who they are in the social groups they belong to is important to adolescents if they are to feel a sense of status. Thus, interventions which focus on the development of interaction skills are necessary.

Here are some suggestions for practice.

IN THERAPY:

- Teach social skills.

- Teach empathic skills.

- Teach assertiveness techniques.

- Carry out a positive self-talk exercise, e.g. with flash cards.

- Teach self-evaluation skills, and help him to identify his strengths.

IN CONSULTATION WITH PARENTS OR CARERS:

- Encourage the child to ask a friend over.
- Involve the child in an activity that he and others value.

IN CONSULTATION WITH SCHOOL STAFF:

- Discuss with the adolescent an area of interest that may raise his social profile.
- Ensure status is obtained, where possible, from a positive act or talent.
- Provide opportunities for the adolescent to practise effective social skills within peer relationships, e.g. through supervised friendship sessions with positive peers, to prevent affiliation with other rejected peers.
- Be vigilant about the risks of bullying – to both victim and perpetrator.

Chapter 6

LAURA

INTRODUCTION

This chapter relates to a case study, Laura, a 16-year-old girl with a high level of anxiety and low self-concept. Laura was one of the participants in my study. The intention of including this in the book is for readers to grasp how human givens can help structure a therapeutic session with a young person, and to give an idea of the types of therapeutic strategies to consider. Information derives from consultations with Laura herself, her mother, form tutor, and psychometrics.

The chapter proceeds by examining the effectiveness of the human givens approach in improving Laura's emotional well-being. Assessment indicated that she had two emotional needs which were problematic for her. These were assessed in more detail and RIGAAR was used to guide the therapeutic process, which included addressing the needs through the employment of a range of interventions in accordance with the human givens APET model.

Background information

Laura was a bright, 16-year-old pupil who attended a secondary school in one of the most deprived areas in the UK. She lived with her mother, father, older sister, and nephew, and reportedly enjoyed her life at home. From the emotional symptoms screening tool, the Beck Youth Inventory, second edition (BYI-II), Laura's score for self-concept placed her within the 'lower than average' range; and for anxiety, the 'moderately elevated' range (Beck, Beck and Jolly 2001).

Laura was identified by school staff as a pupil who:

- was consistently late to form

- often looked withdrawn and tired

- demonstrated poor levels of engagement in class.

Interventions implemented by the school included:

- a behaviour monitoring system

- individual sessions tracking academic progress.

Her school teacher reported that Laura:

- liked individual attention

- was a popular girl, who had a positive peer group in school.

Laura's mother had expressed her concerns to school staff, that Laura:

- was highly anxious about school tasks such as dance performances and reading out in class

- worried that she would let other people down if she made mistakes or failed to meet expectations.

Pre-therapy interview findings indicated that Laura felt the pressure of succeeding, which may have arisen from attending a school which was in a highly socially deprived area, and being the first one in her family considered to have the intelligence to go to university.

Human givens needs

Laura's needs as identified by questions based on the human givens ENA tool (HGI 2007) were:

- autonomy

- privacy.

Laura felt that her emotions, thoughts, and actions were completely controlled by her anxiety. She could not enjoy solitude, as when she was alone she would sabotage the peace with her ruminations, and consequently she avoided her own company.

RECORD OF SESSIONS

Boxes 6.1 to 6.6 outline the activities carried out during therapy sessions.

Box 6.1: Session 1

Plan

- Aim to build Laura's trust — start from an affirmative place.
- Ask Laura for specifics of problem.
- Ask Laura to think about what she would like to gain from therapy — goals.
- Prepare Laura for the end of therapy/discuss likely time scale/number of sessions.

Issues covered and processes worked through
Human givens techniques
RAPPORT BUILDING
Active listening techniques — parroting, paraphrasing, summarizing, reflections.

INFORMATION GATHERING
'Wh' questions, symptom description, activating events, perceptions of others regarding the problem, problem-free talk: what was life like without the problem? The good things and bad things.

GOAL SETTING
Positive, tangible, and achievable.

ACCESSING RESOURCES
Helped Laura to think about the positives of making changes.

Emotional needs and areas covered
AUTONOMY
Transition to high school. Link between emotions, thoughts, and behaviours. Family trip to seaside and planned activities. Fear of failure.

OPPORTUNITIES FOR PRIVACY
Anxiety when alone with thoughts/avoids own company.

Notes

RAPPORT BUILDING AND INFORMATION GATHERING

Laura's trust was built using the rapport-building techniques that permeated the interview. For example, active listening techniques were adopted when Laura was asked what her main concern was, when her anxiety was better or worse, who she was with when her anxiety was better or worse, what she would do when she was anxious, whether this helped or not, and what has helped in the past. Laura's concerns were reflected back to her in order to verify my understanding of her problem. She was asked about the good things, and not so good things, about being anxious, in order to establish factors that may be acting as facilitators and barriers to change. Laura knew that I had listened to her worries; checked that I had heard her concerns correctly; and I had provided her with a sufficient amount of time in which she could convey her feelings, thoughts, and behaviours to me. It was communicated to Laura that she was in control of any change and the amount of change she would make by the end of therapy. To prevent reliance on me as her facilitator of change, an end date of six weeks' time was mentioned.

GOAL SETTING

Laura was asked to think about what she would like to achieve by the end of therapy that she and others would clearly notice.

ACCESSING RESOURCES

Laura was asked about her life as a younger girl, before she became anxious. It was agreed that the only thing holding her back from feeling like this again was the emotions associated with an unplanned family trip, during which she was ill. Laura was given the opportunity to look into the future and see how great her life could be once again, if she allowed it to be.

Box 6.2: Session 2

Plan

- Goal setting.
- Accessing resources.
- Agreeing strategies for change.

Issues covered and processes worked through
Human givens techniques
METAPHOR GENERATION
Laura described her problems in metaphor.

GOAL SETTING
Specifics discussed. Metaphors generated by Laura.

ACCESSING RESOURCES
Laura was reminded of positives of making changes.

AGREEING STRATEGIES
Agreed to explore anxiety and alternative ways of managing it, including the Rewind technique, and distraction, relaxation, and imagery. She was also interested in gaining an understanding of the brain processes relevant to anxiety.

REHEARSAL

- Psychoeducation – controlled worry periods and thought suppression.
- Relaxation and guided imagery.

Emotional needs and areas covered
AUTONOMY
Intrusive thoughts, positive self-talk, and distraction.

OPPORTUNITIES FOR PRIVACY
Anxiety when alone with thoughts.

Notes

METAPHOR GENERATION

Laura described her problem in metaphorical terms, that is, 'I want to be in the driver's seat rather than sat in the back.'

GOAL SETTING

Laura was asked about the goals she wanted to achieve by the end of therapy. She had been asked to think about specifics in between sessions 1 and 2. However, this was difficult for her; therefore, I asked her to think about what she would be doing when she was not anxious, and how would she and other people know she was not anxious. She was given the choice of simply discussing her goals, or drawing them. She presented her goals in pictorial form, completed during the session. They were 'To be happy', represented by a smiley face; 'Being alone can be fun', represented in words only; 'To overcome my problems', represented by a stick person on a ladder; and 'Try to think positively and be in control!', represented by a car with a stick person driving it. Laura provided details of how she might look and be acting if happy, and in control. These were recorded so that I could repeat them during relaxation exercises in forthcoming sessions. (See Figure 6.1.)

ACCESSING RESOURCES

Laura was reminded about her strengths and was encouraged to think about how reducing her anxiety would enable her to be even more of a good listener, good friend, good dancer, and demonstrate her intelligence.

AGREEING STRATEGIES

Laura was given options of how we could proceed to address her needs, through targeting interventions towards her goals. She said she would like to learn about worry postponement, Rewind, distraction, and relaxation techniques. She was quite interested in learning about brain processes and anxiety.

REHEARSAL

Laura was taught the worry postponement technique as her intrusive thoughts prevented her from enjoying being alone, which was one of her goals. She engaged in a relaxation exercise that involved 3/5 breathing techniques and guided imagery. I agreed to record an audio CD, which involved a 3/5 breathing exercise, and a visualization exercise tailored to her fear of participating in the dance exam.

Figure 6.1: Laura's goal setting

Box 6.3: Session 3

Plan

- Find out whether Laura has engaged with therapy – title page and CD homework.
- Determine whether Laura has attended any planned events that have tested her.
- Relaxation exercise.
- Ask Laura if she talked to her mother about the Rewind technique.
- Rewind technique if Laura happy to proceed.

Issues covered and processes worked through

Human givens techniques

RAPPORT BUILDING

Engagement in process? – Title page? Listened to and practised with CD?

INFORMATION GATHERING

Has Laura accessed any testing opportunities?

REHEARSAL

- Relaxation induction.
- Rewind technique.

Emotional needs and areas covered

AUTONOMY

Link between emotions, pattern-matching, thoughts, and behaviours.

OPPORTUNITIES FOR PRIVACY

Practising relaxation alone in bedroom.

Plans for next session

- Title page (see Figure 6.2).
- Rating of Rewind technique.
- Hierarchy of situations that evoke anxiety.
- Creative activity looking at opposite emotions.

Notes

RAPPORT BUILDING

Laura had not brought her title page for this project to the session. This could have indicated that she was not committed to change, and did not want to spend her free time working on tasks aimed at improving her emotional well-being. However, she had practised the relaxation techniques that she had been introduced to last session, using the audio CD 'Relax your way to exam success', which then indeed indicated her commitment to therapy.

INFORMATION GATHERING

I asked Laura about any situations that she had felt anxious about since her last therapeutic session, as I wanted to know if she had been able to put into practice the skills she had learned so far. In fact, she had attended the college open evening on the evening of our session last week. She admitted to being a 'little jittery' but no more than that. Her mother accompanied her, but once there Laura requested to be left alone to talk to teachers, in order to challenge her fear of a planned, novel situation. She signed up for a course. She asserted that she had listened to the relaxation CD before she left for college, and on the car journey there. She was convinced that it was this that had helped her overcome her anxiety.

REHEARSAL

Laura had talked to her mother about the Rewind technique and was happy to proceed. Deep relaxation was induced first, involving a 3/5 breathing exercise and guided imagery. After the Rewind, Laura was asked to rate her feelings about how bothered she was about the event that may have triggered her anxiety, and compare it to how she felt about it before the Rewind.

Figure 6.2: Laura's title page

Box 6.4: Session 4

Plan

- Prepare Laura for the end of therapy.
- Title page.
- Rating of Rewind technique.
- Hierarchy of situations that evoke anxiety.
- Creative activity looking at opposite emotions.
- Celebrations.

Issues covered and processes worked through

Human givens techniques

INFORMATION GATHERING

- Week's ratings of feelings from the Rewind technique.
- Use of relaxation script.
- Hierarchy of worries.

REHEARSAL

- Role play of mock college interview.
- Relaxation in relation to situations reported on the hierarchy of worries.
- Separating the person from the problem – replacing anxiety with humour in creative task.

Emotional needs and areas covered

AUTONOMY

Differences in the level of anxiety experienced depending on the situation. Exuding confidence in an interview situation. Putting anxiety out of the picture.

Plans for next session

- Positive statements about self – flash cards and evidence for them.
- Creative activity concerning experience of therapy.
- Remembering relaxation activities.

Notes

INFORMATION GATHERING

Laura was asked how she would rate her feelings about the event she focused on during the Rewind exercise last week, to establish maintenance of reduction in worry. She had listened to the relaxation CD twice since our last session. At this point, I wanted to appreciate in which situations Laura was continuing to feel anxious, and whether some situations evoked greater anxiety than others. I asked her if she would engage in an exercise called a hierarchy of worries. She decided to undertake this exercise through drawing. I asked her to represent her worries of specific phenomena in the form of a wedding cake with several tiers. The bottom tier, 'having an interview', was her least anxious activity; the second tier was 'going to college'; the third tier was 'performing to an audience'; and the fourth was 'planned trips: day outings'. A copy of Laura's worksheet on the hierarchy of worries activity is shown in Figure 6.3.

Rehearsal

As a result of the hierarchy of worries, Laura and I engaged in a role play of a mock college interview. This exercise tapped into the human givens 'reality generation' notion, that success in a rehearsal situation would most likely lead to success in real life. Laura was asked to think positively about going to college, and she generated three reasons why she should not be overly anxious.

In relation to performing to an audience, in particular her mock GCSE dance exam, relaxation techniques were advised, and she was asked to think about looking past the exam – how could she and others reward her for getting through it, and celebrate her successes? This was to encourage her thinking that the exam period is momentary, and should not control her feelings as much as it was.

Regarding planned trips, Laura was still trying to avoid them. She was asked to challenge herself, when opportunities presented themselves, and to use the techniques she had learned.

Laura engaged in an activity which aimed to help her view the problem as a separate entity, which could be evaluated from a safe distance. In 'Separating the problem from the person', Laura decided to replace anxiety with humour in a creative task. She drew an anxious-looking character, which she named 'Losty', and an opposite, a comical character, which she named 'Bubbly'. She described the actions, feelings, and thoughts of the two characters, in relation to particular situations. Losty was the character who shared the same anxieties Laura did. Bubbly was the character that could be seen having a good laugh when dancing with friends in the studio, and when her nephew tries to eat everything he is given. She said she would like to 'Kick Losty to the Curb!' She would like to be more akin to Bubbly. A copy of Laura's artwork from the 'Separating the problem from the person' exercise is shown in Figure 6.4.

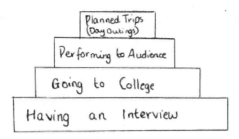

Figure 6.3: Laura's hierarchy of worries

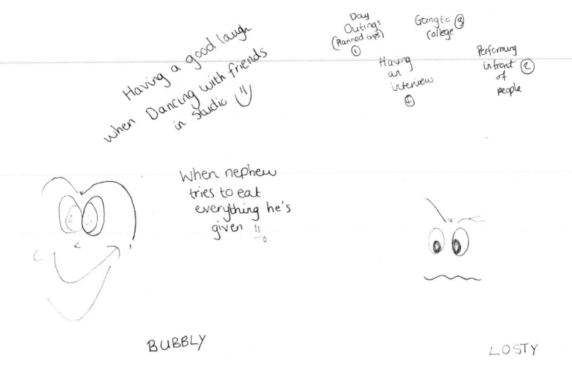

Figure 6.4: Creative activity looking at opposite emotions

Box 6.5: Session 5

Plan

- Prepare Laura for the end of therapy.
- Positive statements about self.
- Reaching goals.
- Relaxing activities worksheet.

Issues covered and processes worked through

Human givens techniques

INFORMATION GATHERING

Situations that have tested Laura.

ACCESSING RESOURCES

Achievements so far.

REHEARSAL

- Positive self-talk and evidence.
- Practised relaxation skills.

Emotional needs and areas covered

AUTONOMY

Link between emotions, pattern-matching, thought, and behaviours.

OPPORTUNITIES FOR PRIVACY

Practising relaxation alone in bedroom.

Plans for next session

- Determining the most and least useful aspects of human givens therapy, and the activities Laura liked and disliked the most.
- Laura to write a letter to another telling them of her successes in therapy.

Notes

INFORMATION GATHERING

Laura was asked about any further situations that she had been tested by since last week. She shared that she had been to her boyfriend's family's party on Saturday evening. She had felt sick and got upset towards lunch time. She practised relaxation techniques using the CD, and visualized going to the party and enjoying herself. She took the pressure off by saying that she did not have to stay if it was too much for her.

ACCESSING RESOURCES

Laura was reminded of how far she had come since starting therapy. Repeating strengths and achievements is a useful means of addressing needs, and indicated to Laura that she was improving her emotional well-being.

REHEARSAL

To maximize the impact of her progress in therapy, an exercise was suggested whereby she would list her achievements so far. She wrote, 'Not letting worry get the better of me in exams'; 'Going to a planned party'; and 'Going to college opening evening and asking lots of questions: felt confident, not scared.' She could remind herself of these achievements on future occasions (see Figure 6.5).

Laura wanted to engage in a positive self-talk exercise, which involved her writing down her strengths. In comparison to the number she recorded in session 2, seven additional strengths were identified, including: 'I am confident', 'I like that I am a good dancer', 'I am good at English'. She provided reasons for each one, which served to increase their authenticity. The statements were written in boxes on A4 card which meant that she could cut them out at home, and use as flash cards. She may refer to these in the future, if her anxiety returns. (See Figure 6.6 for Laura's statements.)

A relaxing activities worksheet was completed by Laura. She was told that she could include activities besides those that she had learned in therapy. She then drew steps and herself as a stick person near the top, to indicate how near she was to completing the goals she set at the beginning of therapy. A copy of Laura's relaxing activities worksheet is shown in Figure 6.7.

Figure 6.5: Laura's achievement – reaching goals

I care about
others a lot
(Friends, Family etc...)

My family are
very loving and
care for me

I am a good
listener

I am in
control of my
own feelings and
thoughts

I have lots
of good friends

I like that
I am friendly
and kind to others.

I am
Confident

I like that I
am a good
dancer

I love the
colour of my
hair

I like that
I have a
Slim build

I am good
at English

Figure 6.6: Laura's positive statements about herself

Figure 6.7: Laura's 'My relaxing activities' worksheet (Stallard 2002)

Box 6.6: Session 6

Plan

- Ask Laura about the most and least useful aspects of human givens therapy, and the activities she liked and disliked the most.
- Laura to write a letter to another about her successes.
- What did she do to reach her goals?
- How does Laura intend to maintain her success?
- What would Laura do if she experienced setbacks in the future?

Issues covered and processes worked through

Therapeutic technique

Letter writing — successes and progress.

Review

Previous five sessions' work.

Emotional needs and areas covered

All previously mentioned.

Notes

THERAPEUTIC TECHNIQUE

Laura was asked if she would like to write a letter to somebody, which would act as an aide memoire of her therapeutic journey, in particular of her achievements, and what she did in order to reach her goals. (See Figure 6.8.)

REVIEW

In order to minimize relapse, Laura was presented with the possibility of situations in the future that may elicit her anxiety, and asked what she would do in those instances. She said she would refer to her file and repeat some of the exercises and techniques she had learned. Laura shared that her favourite parts of therapy were: the guided imagery technique; the college interview role play; and the 'Separating the problem from the person' task. She found all of the relaxation exercises useful, including recording how she likes to relax; the positive self-talk exercise; and the Rewind technique.

Dear Mum,

Since having my sessions I feel like I have gained more confidence and that I am more able to control my anxiety fears/problems. Before I had these sessions I used to get really edgy and nervous about any planned upcoming events, but now I think that I can cope with this a lot better than before. Throughout the weeks I have completed different tasks which I have practised and put into action. Fore example: I have learnt the 3-5 breathing technique which I felt has really helped to calm me down. Secondly, I was lead through the rewind technique which helped me to think about the past and how I could forget about how I used to b (and became much more positive in the future.) I also set myself a list of goals (which I think I have achieved most of them— I am much more happier in myself.) In the sessions, I was able to write down just positive things about myself, which actually helped my confidence (and i can look back at them on cards just to remind myself.) All of these activities and worksheets have really helped me, as just over a month ago I was different than what I am today I can relax myself alot easier than previously, and I am very glad and thankful for the sessions.

Figure 6.8: Laura's letter to her mother following therapy

POST-THERAPY SCORES

Self-concept

Laura's post-therapy outcome score for self-concept placed her within the 'above average' range on the BSCI-Y. This indicated that Laura's self-concept had improved by 14 points in three months.

Anxiety

Laura's post-therapy outcome score for anxiety placed her within the 'average' range on the BAI-Y. This indicated that Laura's anxiety had reduced by 19 points since being assessed three months ago and was a clear improvement.

HOW DID HUMAN GIVENS THERAPY INCREASE LAURA'S EMOTIONAL WELL-BEING?

Positive approach

Laura's emotional improvement was largely accountable to the positive, solution-focused features of human givens therapy, which enabled her to view things from a more realistic perspective; thereby disallowing her to ruminate and engage in self-destructing thoughts. As Seligman (2007) asserts, effects on emotional well-being occur when therapy focuses on building strengths rather than perseverating on past problems.

At post-therapy and follow-up, Laura's presentation was distinctly different to that at pre-therapy.

Her ruminations about her problems were concerning; and there was no knowledge that the therapy would help her 'observing self' take an alternative perspective. However, ruminations turned into solutions and 'what if' had become 'so what' to previously feared events. Laura had been constantly reminded of her past successes, and personal resources.

Taking the lead

Laura was put in complete control as to whether she wanted to practise the skills she had learned in real contexts. She was given options as to how she wanted to experience the Rewind technique, that is, using the visualization method and the TV, or using objects to run through events. She was invited to state a preference for how she wanted to rehearse challenging, real-life situations, for instance through role plays; visualization techniques; talking about her fears and challenging her thoughts; or through drawing activities.

Opportunities to receive attention

Another key theme that came through from Laura's interview was the attention she had received from other people, including her teachers and her mother, when she had dealt with situations in more constructive ways. It appeared that they were surprised at her progress and this was relayed back to Laura. For example, when she went to the party, her mother could not believe that she went in the first place, much less, stayed for the whole evening. She proclaimed 'Wow' to her daughter at her success. She remarked that Laura was going to places for the first time without being sick, for instance the college open evening, and not avoiding or leaving prematurely.

Her mother expressed careful consideration that changes may have occurred as a result of the therapy:

> 'She's looking forward to going to college now. Now I don't know whether that's down to the therapy but I don't know what else it could be. We went to the college open evening and she listened to [her recording of the relaxation script] in the car on the way.'

Before therapy, Laura lacked confidence in carrying out future plans, and stated that therapy had definitely made a difference to her life.

Therapeutic expectations and commitment to change

At the start of human givens therapy, it was made clear to Laura that nothing could be 'done to her' to produce change, and that the key was for herself to engage fully with the therapeutic process, which would take place over six sessions only. It was explained that the people who benefited most from therapy were those who could learn specific techniques in session, and apply them to real-life situations. It was conveyed to Laura that it was majorly important to have faith that a more positive and satisfying life could be achieved by her, and that anxiety is simply an emotion that sometimes becomes wrongly associated with situations that do not need to be appraised as threatening. These explanations may have spurred Laura into the right frame of mind, as she demonstrated commitment to change by practising skills-based techniques such as relaxation and positive self-talk in and outside of sessions, which were corroborated by her mother's reports. Indeed, rehearsing the strategies was one of Laura's strengths. Furthermore, one of the key themes that emerged from the data was a sense of commitment and self-determination in her desire to reduce her anxiety and enjoy life more.

How useful were the employed strategies?

SKILLS-BASED PRACTICE

Laura had referred to tasks involving the visualization of positive outcomes as being the predominant strategy that she used to overcome her fear of the party; the college visit; the mock GCSE exam; and mock college interview with a teacher. However, this may not have been as effective if she had not engaged in the breathing exercises beforehand, as her high emotional arousal would have prevented her from concentrating on the task.

By attending to her needs that were evident in a variety of settings, Laura was helped to learn new ways of experiencing certain situations in session. When it came to real-life events, Laura had created success templates in her mind in therapy, by practising role plays about college interviews and performance exams. Thus, human givens therapy had provided her with the confidence and skills set required to take on opportunities that she feared she would miss as a result of her anxiety. In her own words:

> 'Before I was really worried about my exam but, on the day, I woke up a bit nervous…did my three/five breathing. The night before, I was doing visualizing, imagining myself going into the exam and doing fine, just getting through it and then getting praise after.'

This is a fitting example of how a particular intervention suited Laura's style of learning; was accessible; and her words also give us evidence that she had acquired new skills. Laura emphasized that, before therapy, she would not have been able to go to her dance exam. She reported that she would not have even left the house due to her nerves.

Laura went a step further with her newly found skills and was able to support her friends through the dance performance ordeal: 'Because everyone was worried as well…we were all kinda like in the same boat and we were just reassuring each other.'

Considering Laura's poor subjective well-being before therapy, she had made great progress, evident in the weekly evaluations and the findings from post-therapy data. Scores from the BYI-II indicated that she felt happier, was less anxious, and had greater confidence in her abilities. Therefore, one may hypothesize that the use of the RIGAAR framework and APET model to address Laura's needs were helpful in improving her subjective well-being.

Her worries were no longer affecting her future plans or her daily functioning; and her concerns did not focus on meeting the expectations of others. Laura had learned to reduce her emotional arousal in order to perceive particular situations as non-threatening; remember her previous successes and achievements; and take up further opportunities to experience success. Laura remarked positively on every activity during therapy, apart from the hierarchy of situations. She claimed that she was already aware of her challenges, whereas everything else was new to her.

Human givens therapy had helped Laura to achieve some of the *Every Child Matters* outcomes mentioned in the first chapter, namely being emotionally healthy; enjoying and achieving in school; making a positive contribution by developing self-confidence and dealing with life challenges successfully; and achieving economic well-being by her decision to engage in further education (DfES 2003).

Number of sessions

When considering adolescents with common psychological problems such as anxiety, low self-esteem, and depression, the length of the therapeutic intervention may be a factor in deciding whether or not to take on the work, for instance with the limited capacity faced by many professionals. Brief therapy such as human givens is likely to take a minimum of four sessions in order for the RIGAAR process to be worked through sufficiently. However, one or two further sessions may be more appropriate, as it would allow greater time for naturally occurring, emotion-provoking events to present themselves, and for the adolescent's new skills to be applied to those challenges. Work in sessions could then be used to address current real-life issues. Sessions could also be delivered on a fortnightly basis rather than weekly.

REFERENCES

Abramson, L., Seligman, M. and Teasdale, J. (1978) 'Learned helplessness in humans: Critique and reformulation.' *Journal of Abnormal Psychology 87*, 49–74.

Achenbach, T.M., McConaughy, S.H. and Howell, C.T. (1987) 'Child adolescent behavioural and emotional problems: Implications of cross-informant correlations for situational specificity.' *Psychological Bulletin 101*, 213–232.

Ahrens-Eipper, S. and Hoyer, J. (2006) 'Applying the Clark–Wells model of social phobia to children: The case of a dictation phobia.' *Behavioural and Cognitive Psychotherapy 34*, 1, 103–106.

Ainsworth, M.D.S., Blehar, M., Walls, S. and Walters, E. (1978) *Patterns of Attachment*. Hillsdale, NJ: Erlbaum.

Atkinson, C. (2008) *Human Givens: Relaxation* [handout]. Unpublished course unit resource for Doctorate in Educational and Child Psychology. Manchester: University of Manchester.

Atkinson, C. and Woods, K. (2003) 'Motivational Interviewing strategies for disaffected secondary school students: A case example.' *Educational Psychology in Practice 19*, 1, 49–64.

Aubrey, L.L. (1998) *Motivational Interviewing with Adolescents Presenting for Outpatient Substance Abuse Treatment*. Doctoral dissertation, University of New Mexico.

Bachelor, A. and Horvath, A. (2006) 'The Therapeutic Relationship.' In M.A. Hubble, B.L. Duncan and S.D. Miller (eds) *The Heart and Soul of Change: What Works in Therapy*. Washington, DC: American Psychological Association.

Baginsky, W. (2004) *School Counselling in England, Wales and Northern Ireland: A Review*. London: National Society for the Prevention of Cruelty to Children.

Bandler, R. (1985) *Using Your Brain for a Change*. Colorado: Real People Press.

Bandura, A. (1997) *Self-Efficacy*. New York: Freeman.

Baxter, J. and Frederickson, N. (2005) 'Every Child Matters: Can educational psychology contribute to radical reform?' *Educational Psychology in Practice 21*, 2, 87–102.

Beck, J., Beck, A. and Jolly, J. (2001) *Beck Youth Inventories*. New York: The Psychological Corporation.

Benazon, N.R., Ager, J. and Rosenberg, D.R. (2002) 'Cognitive Behaviour Therapy in treatment-naive children and adolescents with Obsessive-Compulsive Disorder: An open trial.' *Behaviour Research 40*, 529–539.

Boscarino, J.A. (1996) 'Posttraumatic stress disorder, exposure to combat, and lower plasma cortisol among Vietnam veterans: Findings and clinical implications.' *Journal of Consulting and Clinical Psychology 64*, 191–201.

Bostic, K.E. and Everall, R.D. (2006) 'In my mind I was alone: Suicidal adolescents' perceptions of attachment relationships.' *International Journal for the Advancement of Counselling 28*, 3, 269–287.

Bowlby, J. (1969) *Attachment and Loss: Attachment* Vol. I. London: Hogarth.

Bowlby, J. (1969/1982) *Attachment and Loss: Loss*. Vol. I. New York: Basic Books.

Bowlby, J. (1988) *A Secure Base: Clinical Applications of Attachment Theory*. London: Hogarth Press.

Briere, J. (1995) *Trauma Symptom Checklist for Children*. Florida: Psychological Assessment Resources.

British Psychological Society (2006) *Ethical Guidelines and Support*. Accessed on 18/11/10 at www.bps.org.uk/the-society/code-of-conduct/code-of-conduct_home.cfm.

Burns, G.W. (2005) *101 Healing Stories for Kids and Teens*. Chichester: Wiley.

Carr, A. (2004) *Positive Psychology: The Science of Happiness and Human Strengths*. London: Brunner-Routledge.

Carr, A. (2006) *The Handbook of Child and Adolescent Clinical Psychology: A Contextual Approach* (2nd edition). London and New York: Routledge.

Chua, S.N. and Koestner, R. (2008) 'A self-determination theory perspective on the role of autonomy in solitary behavior.' *The Journal of Social Psychology 148*, 5, 645–647.

Colligan, R.P. (1999) *Education Counselling Service: Best Value Review*. Dudley: Dudley Metropolitan Borough Consultation Paper.

Collishaw, S., Maughan, B., Goodman, R. and Pickles, A. (2004) 'Time trends in adolescent mental health.' *Journal of Child Psychology and Psychiatry 45*, 8, 1350–1362.

Cooper, M. (2009) 'Counselling in UK secondary schools: A comprehensive review of audit and evaluation studies.' *Counselling and Psychotherapy Research 9*, 3, 137–150.

Cooper, M., Rowland, N., McArthur, K., Pattison, S., Cromarty, K. and Richards, K. (2010) 'Humanistic counselling for emotional distress in young people: Feasibility study and preliminary indications of efficacy.' *Child and Adolescent Psychiatry and Mental Health 4*, 12, 1–12.

Costa, P. and McCrae, P. (1992) *Revised NEO Personality Inventory (NEO-PI-R) and NEO Five-Factor Inventory (NEO-FFI)*. Professional Manual. Odessa, Florida: Psychological Assessment Resources.

Crane, P.A. and Clements, P.T. (2005) 'Psychological responses to disaster: Focus on adolescents.' *Journal of Psychosocial Nursing 43*, 8, 31–38.

Currie, C., Roberts, C., Morgan, A., Smith, R. *et al*. (2004) *Young People's Health in Context: Health Behaviour in School-aged Children (HBSC) Study: International Report from the 2001/2002 Survey*. Copenhagen: WHO Publications.

Currie, J.F. (2001) 'Specific psychotherapies for childhood and adolescent depression: The unmet needs in diagnosis and treatment of mood disorders in children and adolescents.' *Biological Psychiatry 49*, 12, 1091–1100.

Dallos, R. (2003) 'Using narrative and attachment theory in systemic family therapy with eating disorders.' *Clinical Child Psychology and Psychiatry 8*, 521–537.

Davis, H., Day, C., Cox, A. and Cutler, L. (2000) 'Child and adolescent mental health needs: Assessment and service implications in an inner city area.' *Clinical Child Psychology and Psychiatry 5*, 2, 169–188.

Deci, E. and Ryan, R. (2002) *Handbook of Self-Determination Research*. Rochester, NY: University of Rochester Press.

Dennison, C. (1998) *An Evaluation of the Brighton and Hove Joint Action Consortium School Counselling Project*. Brighton: Trust for the Study of Adolescence.

Department for Children, Schools and Families (2008) *Targeted Mental Health in Schools*. Nottingham: DCSF.

Department for Education and Skills (2001) *Promoting Children's Mental Health within Early Years and School Settings*. Nottingham: DfES Publications.

Department for Education and Skills (2003) *Every Child Matters*. Nottingham: DFES Publications.

Department of Health (2004) *National Healthy Schools Programme*. London: DH Publications.

Department of Health (2008) *Improving Access to Psychological Therapies*. National Institute for Mental Health in England. Accessed on 18/08/10 at www.dh.gov.uk.

De Shazer, S. (1985) *Keys to Solution in Brief Therapy*. New York: W.W. Norton.

DeVries, B., Van der Meij, H. and Lazonder, A.W. (2008) 'Supporting reflective web searching in elementary schools.' *Computers in Human Behavior 24*, 3, 649–665.

Dozier, M., Cue, K. and Barnett, L. (1994) 'Clinicians as caregivers: The role of attachment organization in treatment.' *Journal of Consulting and Clinical Psychology 62*, 793–800.

Dunsmuir, S. and Iyadurai, S. (2007) 'Cognitive Behavioural Therapy: Effectiveness, expertise and ethics.' *Division of Educational and Child Psychology: Debate 122*, 15–19.

Durrant, M. (1995) *Creative Strategies for School Problems*. New York: Norton.

Eckes, A. and Radunovich, H.L. (2007) *Trauma and Adolescents*. Department of Family, Youth and Community Sciences, University of Florida. Accessed on 18/11/10 at https://edis.ifas.ufl.edu/fy1004.

Ehntholt, K.A., Smith, P.A. and Yule, W. (2005) 'School-based cognitive-behavioural therapy group intervention for refugee children who have experienced war-related trauma.' *Clinical Child Psychology and Psychiatry 10*, 2, 235–250.

Eisenberg, N., Fabes, R.A., Karbon, M. and Murphy, B. (1996) 'The relations of children's dispositional empathy-related responding to their emotionality, regulation, and social functioning.' *Developmental Psychology 32*, 195–209.

Ellis, A. (1991) 'The revised ABC's of Rational-Emotive Therapy.' *Journal of Rational-Emotive and Cognitive-Behavior Therapy 9*, 3, 139–172.

Evidence-Based Mental Health Online (EBMH) (2008) *Review. Psychotherapy for Adolescents with Depression: Initial but No Sustainable Benefits*. Accessed on 10.04.08 at http://ebmh.bmj.com.

Farrell, P., Woods, K., Lewis, S., Rooney, S. *et al.* (2006) *A Review of the Functions and Contribution of Educational Psychologists in England and Wales in the Light of Every Child Matters: Change for Children*. Nottingham: Department for Education and Employment.

Feeney, J. and Noller, P. (1996) *Adult Attachment*. Thousand Oaks, CA: Sage.

Fox, H. (2010) *When 6 is Bigger Than 10: Unmasking Anorexia Through Externalisation*. London: The Institute of Narrative Therapy. Papers and resources. Accessed on 21/08/10 at www.theinstituteofnarrativetherapy.com/Papers%20and%20resources.html.

Freud, S. (1912) 'The Dynamics of Transference.' In *The Standard Edition of the Complete Psychological Works of Sigmund Freud*. London: Hogarth Press.

Friedberg, R. and McClure, J. (2002) 'Clinical Practice of Cognitive Therapy with Children and Adolescents.' In A. Carr (ed.) *The Handbook of Child and Adolescent Clinical Psychology: A Contextual Approach* (2nd edition). London and New York: Routledge.

Gollop, A. and Pulley, C. (2010) *Documenting Children's Stories*. Accessed on 21/08/10 at www.theinstituteofnarrativetherapy.com/Papers%20and%20resources.html.

Goodman, R. (1997) 'The Strengths and Difficulties Questionnaire: A research note.' *Journal of Child Psychology and Psychiatry 38*, 581–586.

Green, H., McGinnity, A., Meltzer, H., Ford, T. and Goodman, R. (2005) *Mental Health of Children and Young People in Great Britain, 2004: National Statistics*. Accessed on 30/10/09 at www.ic.nhs.uk/webfiles/publications/mentalhealth04/MentalHealthChildrenYoungPeople310805_PDF.pdf.

Greenberger, D. and Padesky, C.A. (1995) *Mind Over Mood: Change How You Feel by Changing the Way You Think*. New York: Guilford Press.

Griffin, J. (2008) *How to do Effective Counselling*. Unpublished course unit resource for DEdChPsy Doctorate in Educational and Child Psychology. Manchester: Manchester University.

Griffin, J. and Tyrrell, I. (2007) *Human Givens: A New Approach to Emotional Health and Clear Thinking*. East Sussex: HG Publishing.

Grotberg, E.H. (2003) *Resilience for Today: Gaining Strength from Adversity*. Connecticut: Praeger Publishers.

Hafen, B., Karren, K., Frandsen, K. and Smith, N. (1996) *Mind/body Health: The Effects of Attitudes, Emotions, and Relationships*. Boston, MA: Allyn and Bacon.

Hales, R.E. and Yudofsky, S.C. (2003) *The American Psychiatric Publishing Textbook of Clinical Psychiatry* (4th edition). Arlington, VA: American Psychiatric Publishing.

Hamblen, J. (2010) *Hidden Hurt: Domestic Abuse Information*. PTSD in Children and Adolescents. Accessed on 20/08/10 at www.hiddenhurt.co.uk/Articles/PTSDkids.htm.

Horvath, A.O. and Symonds, B.D. (1991) 'Relation between working alliance and outcome in psychotherapy: A meta-analysis.' *Journal of Counselling Psychology 38*, 139–149.

Howe, D. (1995) *Attachment Theory for Social Work Practice*. Basingstoke: Macmillan.

Howe, D., Brandon, M., Hinings, D. and Schofield, G. (1999) *Attachment Theory, Child Maltreatment and Family Support.* Basingstoke: Macmillan.

Howes, C. (1999) 'Attachment Relationships in the Context of Multiple Caregivers.' In J. Cassidy and P.R. Shaver (eds) *Handbook of Attachment.* New York: Milford Press.

Howes, C. and Smith, E.W. (1995) 'Relations between child-care quality, teacher behavior, children's play activities, emotional security, and cognitive activity in child care.' *Early Childhood Research Quarterly 10,* 381–404.

Human Givens Institute (2007) *Emotional Needs Audit Tool.* Accessed on 11/08/10 at www.enaproject.org.

Human Givens Institute (2010) *Professional Register of Qualified HG Therapists in Private Practice.* Accessed on 21/08/10 at www.hgi.org.uk/register/index.htm.

Human Givens Practice Research Network (HGIPRN) (2009) *Evidence-based Therapy.* Accessed on 15/08/10 at www.hgiprn.org.

Jablonska, L. and Lindberg, L. (2007) 'Risk behaviours, victimization and mental distress among adolescents in different family structures.' *Social Psychiatry and Psychiatric Epidemiology 42,* 656–663.

Jackson, S. and Parnham, B. (1996) 'Evaluation of an Independent Counselling Service in Schools.' Unpublished report for NSPCC. In P. Jenkins and F. Polat (eds) *The Current Provision of Counselling Services in Secondary Schools in England and Wales.* Manchester: University of Manchester.

Jenkins, P. and Polat, F. (eds) (2005) *The Current Provision of Counselling Services in Secondary Schools in England and Wales.* Manchester: University of Manchester.

Kendall, P.C. (1994) 'Treating anxiety disorders in children: Results of a randomized clinical trial.' *Journal of Consulting and Clinical Psychology 62,* 1, 100–110.

Kennedy, J.H. and Kennedy, C.E. (2004) 'Attachment theory: Implications for school psychology.' *Psychology in the Schools 41,* 2, 247–259.

Kurtz, Z., Thornes, R. and Wolkind, S. (1994) *Services for the Mental Health of Children and Young People in England: A National Review.* London: Maudsley Hospital and South Thames Regional Health Authority.

Lambert, M.J. (1992) 'Implications of Outcome Research for Psychotherapy Integration.' In M.A. Hubble, B.L. Duncan and S.D. Miller (eds) *The Heart and Soul of Change: What Works in Therapy.* Washington, DC: American Psychological Society.

Lambert, M.J. and Anderson, E.M. (1996) 'Assessment for the time-limited psychotherapies.' *Annual Review of Psychiatry 15,* 23–47.

Larsson, B., Daleflod, L. and Hakansson, L. (1987) 'Therapist-assisted versus self-help relaxation treatment of chronic headaches in adolescents: A school-based intervention.' *Journal of Child Psychology and Psychiatry 28,* 127–136.

LeDoux, J.E. (1998) *The Emotional Brain.* New York: Weidenfeld and Nicolson.

Maslow, A.H. (1943) 'A theory of human motivation.' *Psychological Review 50,* 4, 370–396.

Mayo, E. (1933) *The Human Problems of an Industrial Civilisation.* Basingstoke: Macmillan.

McGrath, P.A. and Holahan, A.L. (2004) 'Psychological interventions with children and adolescents: Evidence for their effectiveness in treating chronic pain.' *Seminars in Pain Medicine 1,* 2, 99–109.

McNamara, E. (1998) *The Theory and Practice of Eliciting Pupil Motivation: Motivational Interviewing – A Form Teacher's Manual and Guide for Students, Parents, Psychologists, Health Visitors and Counsellors.* Merseyside: Positive Behaviour Management.

Meltzer, H., Gartward, R., Ford, T. and Goodman, R. (2000) *Mental Health of Children and Adolescents in Great Britain.* London: The Stationery Office.

Metcalf, L. (1995) *Counselling Towards Solutions: A Practical Solution Focused Program for Working with Students, Teachers and Parents.* New Jersey: Simon and Schuster.

Miller, W.R., Westerberg, V.S., and Waldron, H.B. (2003) 'Evaluating Alcohol Problems in Adults and Adolescents.' In R.K. Hester and W.R. Miller (eds) *Handbook of Alcoholism Treatment Approaches: Effective Alternatives* (3rd edition). Boston, MA: Allyn and Bacon.

Mindfields College (2007) *The Human Givens Diploma Course* (14th edition). Chalvington, East Sussex: HG Publishing.

Murphy, J. and Duncan, B. (1997) *Brief Intervention for School Problems: Collaborating for Practical Solutions.* New York: Guilford Press.

National Institute for Clinical Excellence (NICE) (2005) *Depression in Children and Young People.* Accessed on 23/10/09 at www.nice.org.uk/nicemedia/pdf/cg028fullguideline.pdf.

Noble, T. and McGrath, H. (2008) 'The positive educational practices framework: A tool for facilitating the work of educational psychologists in promoting pupil well-being.' *Educational and Child Psychology 25*, 2, 119–134.

Piaget, J. (1932) *The Moral Judgement of the Child.* New York: Free Press.

Pianta, R.C. and Steinberg, M.S. (1992) 'Teacher–Child Relationships and Adjusting to School.' In R.C. Pianta (ed.) *New Directions in Child Development. Beyond the Parent: The Role of Other Adults in Children's Lives.* San Francisco: Jossey Bass.

Public Health Emergency (PHE) (2005) *Helping Children and Adolescents Cope with Violence and Disasters.* Accessed on 26/08/10 at www.phe.gov/emergency/communication/guides/media/Documents/14j.pdf.

Redpath, D. and Harker, M. (1998) 'Becoming solution-focused in practice.' *Educational Psychology in Practice 15*, 2, 116–121.

Renou, J. (2010) *A Study of Perceptual Learning Styles and Achievement in a University-level Foreign Language Course.* Accessed on 24/08/10 at http://crisolenguas.uprrp.edu/Articles/JanetRenou.pdf.

Rhodes, J. and Ajmal, Y. (1995) *Solution Focused Thinking in Schools.* London: B.T. Press.

Richards, A., Rivers, I. and Akhurst, J. (2008) 'A positive psychology approach to tackling bullying in secondary schools: A comparative evaluation.' *Educational and Child Psychology 25*, 2, 72–81.

Rogers, C. (1961) *On Becoming a Person: The Struggle Toward Self-Realisation.* London: Constable.

Rogers, C. (1976) *Client Centred Therapy.* London: Constable.

Rollnick, S. and Miller, W.R. (1995) 'What is motivational interviewing?' *Behavioural and Cognitive Psychotherapy 23*, 325–334.

Rollnick, S., Heather, N. and Bell, A. (1992) 'Negotiating behaviour change in medical settings: The development of brief motivational interviewing.' *Journal of Mental Health 1*, 25–37.

Roth, A. and Fonagy, P. (2006) *What Works for Whom.* New York: Guilford Press.

Rotter, J.B. (1966) 'Generalized expectancies for internal versus external control of reinforcement.' *Psychological Monographs 80*, 1–28.

Rutter, M., Kim-Cohen, J. and Maughan, B. (2006) 'Continuities and discontinuities in psychopathology between childhood and adult life.' *Journal of Child Psychology and Psychiatry 47*, 3/4, 276–295.

Seeman, T.E. and Syme, S.L. (1987) 'Social networks and coronary heart disease: A comparison of the structure and function of social relations as predictors of disease.' *Psychosomatic Medicine 49*, 4, 341–354.

Selekman, M. (1993) *Pathways to Change: Brief Therapy Solutions with Difficult Adolescents.* New York: Guilford Press.

Seligman, M.E.P. (1975) *Helplessness: On Depression, Development, and Death.* San Francisco: W.H. Freeman.

Seligman, M.E.P. (1998) *Learned Optimism: How to Change Your Mind and Your Life* (2nd edition). New York: Pocket Books.

Seligman, M. (2000) 'Positive Clinical Psychology.' In L.G. Aspinwall and U.M. Staudinger (eds) *A Psychology of Human Strengths: Perspectives on an Emerging Field.* Washington, DC: American Psychological Association.

Seligman, M.E.P. (2003) *Authentic Happiness: Understanding the New Positive Psychology to Realize Your Potential for Lasting Fulfillment.* London: Nicholas Brealey.

Seligman, M.E.P. (2007) *Positive Psychology, Positive Prevention, and Positive Therapy.* Accessed on 07/04/08 at www.ppc.sas.upenn.edu/ppsnyderchapter.htm.

Seligman, M.E.P., Steen, T.A., Park, N. and Peterson, C. (2005) 'Positive psychology progress: Empirical validation of interventions.' *American Psychologist 60*, 5, 410–421.

Shaw, J. (2000) 'Children, adolescents and trauma.' *Psychiatric Quarterly 71*, 3, 227–243.

Silove, D., Steel, Z. and Psychol, M. (2006) 'Understanding community psychological response after disasters: Implications for mental health services.' *Journal of Postgraduate Medicine 52*, 121–125.

Siqueland, L., Rynn, M. and Diamond, G.S. (2005) 'Cognitive behavioural and attachment based family therapy for anxious adolescents: Phase I and II studies.' *Journal of Anxiety Disorders 19*, 4, 361–381.

Sladden, J. (2005) 'Psychotherapy skills in the real world.' *BMJ Career Focus 330*, 33–35.

Squires, G. (2001) 'Thoughts, feelings, behaviour: Helping children understand themselves and take more control of their behaviour.' *Special Children 134*, 15–18.

Stallard, P. (2002) *Think Good – Feel Good: A Cognitive Behaviour Therapy Workbook for Children and Young People.* Chichester: Wiley.

Strupp, H.H. (1980) 'Success and failure in time-limited psychotherapy.' *Archives of General Psychiatry 27*, 595–603.

Twigg, E., Barkham, M., Bewick, B.M., Mulhern, B. *et al.* (2009) 'The Young Person's CORE: Development of a brief outcome measure for young people.' *Counselling and Psychotherapy Research 9*, 3, 160–168.

United Nations Children's Fund (UNICEF) (2007) *Child Poverty in Perspective: An Overview of Child Well-being in Rich Countries.* Florence: Innocenti Research Centre.

Vaiva, G., Ducrocq, F., Jezequel, K. and Averland, B. *et al.* (2003) 'Immediate treatment with propranolol decreases posttraumatic stress disorder two months after trauma.' *Biological Psychiatry 54*, 9, 947–949.

Van Vlierberghe, L.V. and Braet, C. (2007) 'Dysfunctional schemas and psychopathology in referred obese adolescents.' *Clinical Psychology and Psychotherapy 14*, 342–351.

Vetere, A. and Dowling, E. (eds) (2005) *Narrative Therapies with Children and Their Families: A Practitioner's Guide to Concepts and Approaches.* London: Routledge.

Villalba, J.A. and Lewis, L.D. (2007) 'Children, adolescents, and isolated traumatic events: Counseling considerations for couples and family counselors.' *The Family Journal 15*, 30–35.

Waller, G. (2000) 'Mechanisms underlying binge eating.' *European Eating Disorders Review 8*, 347–350.

Weikle, J.E. (1993) *Self-talk and Self-health.* Accessed on 01/03/09 at www.ericdigests.org/1994/self.htm.

Wells, A. (2003) *Cognitive Therapy of Anxiety Disorders: A Practice Manual and Conceptual Guide.* Chichester: Wiley.

Wheeler, R. (2006) 'Gillick or Fraser? A plea for consistency over competence in children.' *British Medical Journal 332*, 7545, 815–837.

White, M. and Epston, D. (1990) *Narrative Means to Therapeutic Ends.* New York: Norton.

Wilcox, E. and Whittington, A. (2003) 'Discovering the use of narrative metaphors in work with people with learning disabilities.' *Clinical Psychology 21*, 31–35.

World Health Organization (WHO) (1993) *The Health of Young People: A Challenge and a Promise.* Accessed on 26/08/10 at www.searo.who.int/LinkFiles/Initiatives_AHD_in_Nepal.pdf.

Yates, Y. (2008) *Human Givens Therapy and Emotional Well-being in Adolescents. An Introduction.* North West Educational Psychology CPD conference, Chorley, UK.

Yates, Y. (2009a) *Human Givens Therapy and Subjective Well-being in Adolescents.* Inclusion Service Development Day, Warrington Local Authority, UK.

Yates, Y. (2009b) *Human Givens Therapy and Subjective Well-being in Adolescents.* North West Educational Psychology CPD Conference, Chorley, UK.

Yates, Y. (2009c) 'Relax your way to exam success' [CD]. Available from www.ypspsychology.co.uk/Products.html (2011 education catalogue 'Incentive Plus').

Yates, Y. and Atkinson, C. (in press) 'Using human givens therapy to support the well-being of adolescents: A case example.' *Pastoral Care in Education.*

Zeider, M. and Endler, N. (1996) *Handbook of Coping: Theory, Research, Applications.* New York: Wiley.

Zeller, M.H., Saelens, B.E., Kirk, S., Roehrig, H. *et al.* (2004) 'Psychological adjustment of obese youth presenting for weight management treatment.' *Obesity Research 12*, 1576–1586.

SUBJECT INDEX

AUTHOR INDEX